THE IMPORTANCE OF
Worshiping
TOGETHER

Textbook Series

THE IMPORTANCE OF
Worshiping
TOGETHER

VITAL BIBLICAL DYNAMICS FOR UNIFIED WORSHIP

Shamblin Stone

LifeRich Publishing is a registered trademark of The Reader's Digest Association, Inc.

LifeRich Publishing books may be ordered through booksellers or by contacting:

LifeRich Publishing
1663 Liberty Drive
Bloomington, IN 47403
www.liferichpublishing.com
1 (888) 238-8637

ISBN: 978-1-4897-2865-4 (sc)
ISBN: 978-1-4897-2864-7 (hc)
ISBN: 978-1-4897-2866-1 (e)

Library of Congress Control Number: 2020906975

Print information available on the last page.

LifeRich Publishing rev. date: 05/22/2020

Dedicated to the memory of
my parents

Rev. Ralph Shamblin and Willa B. Stone

CONTENTS

LIST OF PICTURES AND ILLUSTRATIONS

LIST OF TABLES

PREFACE

"YOU CAN'T KILL A DEAD MAN"

THE BIBLICAL WORSHIP TEXTBOOK SERIES

You are reading the third book in a series that contains what God has taught me about Christian worship from the Bible. These books are:

1. Stone, Shamblin. *Biblical Worship: God Has Always Had a Way He Wants to Be Worshiped*. Bloomington, Indiana: Westbow Press, 2012.

This book covers general aspects about worship and establishes that God has the right to tell us how, when, and where He wants us to worship Him.

2. Stone, Shamblin. *Portrait of a Worshiper: How God Designed and Created Us to Fulfill Our Purpose.* Bloomington, Indiana: Westbow Press, 2018.

This book shows us that the way God designed and created us as human beings makes it possible for us to accomplish the purpose for which He created us, which is to worship Him. It is about worship from an individual perspective.

3. Stone, Shamblin. *The Importance of Worshiping Together: Vital Biblical Dynamics for Unified Worship.* Bloomington, Indiana: LifeRich Publishing, 2020.

This book introduces the biblical reasons for group worship and addresses some of the major threats against unity in worship. It is about worship from a sociological perspective.

4. Stone, Shamblin. *Leading Worship: Biblical and Practical Principles of Worship Leading*, to be published.

This book will outline the Biblical qualifications for worship leaders, since God has made it clear that the gatherings of the church must always have leadership. It will also introduce the Biblical patterns of worship and apply them to the various practical aspects of leading worship.

5. Stone, Shamblin. *Biblical and Contemporary Worship Teams: How Biblical Worship Team Configurations Apply Today*, to be published.

This book will examine the various Biblical worship team configurations and apply them to the practicalities of serving on a worship team in today's church.

When the Lord began teaching me about worship back in the late 1970s, He made it clear that He would only reveal to me about ten percent of what He wanted His church to know about worship. These books are my attempt to be obedient to God to share the revelation knowledge I have received from Him about worship. I am also anxious to learn the other ninety percent from others whom God has given revelation about worship.

The prefaces of these books are not introductions to the worship teachings found in each book but rather to me. In the first book of this series, *Biblical Worship*, the preface was entitled "My Call to Teach Worship." It is about the God-directed transformation in my life from a singer/songwriter and performing artist to that of someone who wanted, above all else, to help local churches experience Biblical worship for themselves.

In "How I Committed Suicide," the preface to *Portrait of a Worshiper*, I share my testimony of how I gave my life to Jesus Christ and the circumstances that led up to that event.

Now, in this book's preface, I would like to talk about the time in my life between when I was saved in Da Nang, Vietnam, to the time when God redirected my ministry from performance to worship.

In other words:

➢ The preface of book two of this series contains part one of my testimony.

➤ The preface in book three of this series contains part two of my testimony.

➤ The preface in book one of this series contains part three of my testimony.

➤ The preface(s) in book(s) four and five will talk about the many miracles God has done over the course of our lives.

The preface you are reading now contains my stories and Bible teaching. The teaching here addresses a fundamental aspect of a Christian's relationship with the Lord Jesus and is included to Biblically validate the experiences I am sharing.

HOW I "COMMITTED SUICIDE"

Here is an overview of the last thing I shared in the preface of *Portrait of a Worshiper*.

In 1970 I "committed suicide" in Da Nang, Vietnam when Don Elliot found me in my room as I was contemplating the best way to kill myself. He said he had a good way for me to do it, so I listened to him as he read me this Bible verse.

> *For whosoever will save his life shall lose it: and whosoever will lose his life for* **My** *sake shall find it. Matthew 16:25 (KJV) emphasis added*

"If you want to kill yourself," Don said, holding his open New Testament out to me, "do it this way. Give your life to Jesus and you will find out what life is meant to be about."

So, I "killed myself." I gave Jesus every part of my messed-up life, and He has kept His word to me. He has revealed to me the purpose He gave to all human life, which can be summed up by these two verses:

> *. . . that we who first trusted in Christ should be to the praise of His glory. Ephesians 1:12 (NKJV)*

> *This people have I formed for Myself. They shall show forth My praise. Isaiah 43:21 (KJV)*

Paul understood what it meant to be a walking dead man as well. We learn that from these scripture verses:

> *I have been crucified with Christ; it is no longer I who live, but Christ lives in me; and the* life *which I now live in the flesh I live by faith in the Son of God, who loved me and gave Himself for me. Galatians 2:20 (NKJV)*

> *I beseech you therefore, brethren, by the mercies of God, that you present your bodies a living sacrifice, holy, acceptable to God, which is your reasonable service. Romans 12:1 (NKJV)*

> *I affirm, by the boasting in you which I have in Christ Jesus our Lord, I die daily. 1 Corinthians 15:31 (NKJV)*

A dead man doesn't have to impress anyone. A dead man can do nothing on his own. A dead man has no rights. A dead man is simply dead. But a dead man that is walking around by the life of Christ as if he is alive can easily be mistaken for a living man, unless something happens to prove the man is dead.

This is what happened to me on August 5th, 1975. I was shot at point-blank range. The bullet clipped the major vein, my vena cava, which returns blood back to the heart. The doctors said I had no blood in my blood vessels by the time they got to me. They said I had completely bled out into my body cavity. I should have been dead.

But I am getting ahead of myself. Let me first tell you a few things that led up to that event.

HOW GOD TALKS TO MAN

If you do not understand that God speaks to man, you will have trouble accepting my testimony. I have inserted this short teaching segment to help you with this principle.

Even if you do not want to accept this Biblical principle, the fact remains that it is possible for a human being to carry on a conversation with God. It is my belief that not only can we speak to God and have

Him respond to us Spirit to spirit, or even audibly at times, but that this should be the normal relationship between all of us and God. This type of relationship between God and man is verified throughout the Bible. Here are just a few examples to show you what I mean.

1. The Lord spoke audibly.

    *After this I looked, and, behold, a door was opened in heaven: and the first voice which **I heard** was as it were of a trumpet talking with me; which said, Come up hither, and I will shew thee things which must be hereafter. Revelation 4:1 (KJV) emphasis added*

2. This next conversation went on in Paul's spirit and mind.

    *For this thing I besought the Lord thrice, that it might depart from me. And **He said** unto me, My grace is sufficient for thee: for My strength is made perfect in weakness… 2 Corinthians 12:8-9 (KJV) emphasis added*

3. Finally, this conversation happened in a vision.

    *And there was a certain disciple at Damascus, named Ananias; and to him said the Lord **in a vision**, Ananias. And he said, Behold, I am here, Lord. And **the Lord said** unto him, Arise, and go into the street which is called Straight, and enquire in the house of Judas for one called Saul, of Tarsus: for, behold, he prayeth. Acts 9:10-11 (KJV) emphasis added*

I have experienced God talk to me in these three ways. God does talk to His people. This is even confirmed by Jesus Himself.

My sheep hear My voice, and I know them, and they follow Me. John 10:27 (KJV)

If you are one of Jesus' sheep, you hear His voice whether you recognize it or not. Jesus always speaks to His sheep. The fact that Jesus speaks to

His people is presumed in this statement. Nobody would hear Jesus speak if He were not speaking. Jesus said that every one of His sheep hear His voice. The problem is that many of us have never learned how to recognize His voice.

Most people misquote this verse and say, "My sheep know My voice." But that is not what Jesus said. Unfortunately, a lot of people do not "know" God's voice when He speaks, and they get nervous around Christians who say they have heard God speak to them because they do not understand that this happens.

THE POWER OF MUSIC

A couple of months after I gave my life to Christ in Da Nang, I attended a USO concert at the base theater. Although it was a secular music group, God opened my eyes in that concert to see the spiritual power He has built into music. Following the concert, although the other GIs were leaving the theater, I sat in my seat overwhelmed by this new revelation concerning music.

USO Concert at Da Nang Air Force Base Theater (Fall 1970)

What happened next was the first time I had experienced God talking to me. I believe it happened in a vision. Although it was totally new to me, it felt natural. It felt to me like this is the way God communicates with man.

"Do you like what I have shown you about music?" God interrupted my contemplation.

"You better believe I do," I responded to Him. "I had no idea You made music so powerful!"

"Good." God smiled. "Because that's what I have called you to do!"

"Music?"

"That's right," God affirmed.

"Wow . . ."

Da Nang Folk Gospel Trio

Before I knew it, I was singing in a Christian folk trio. We had three-part harmony, two guitars, and a standup bass. We mainly sang in the base hospital for the severely wounded GIs, but the chapel had us perform a full concert around Christmas time. Our bass player received orders to leave Da Nang in January, so the trio discontinued.

Da Nang Gospel Quartet

By February I was in an a cappella male quartet. We sang for many chapel sponsored events, like cookouts, as well as the chapel services. We stayed together until I received orders to leave Da Nang that April.

Upon returning to the States, I was stationed at McConnell Air Force Base near Wichita, Kansas. I was singing solo concerts with my guitar in many different churches, youth groups, and chapel services and had hooked up with two other musicians to form a musical group. Steve Alexander was in the air force, and Rod Ellis had moved to Wichita from Kansas City to form the group with us. Rod played a Martin guitar, I played a Yamaha 12-string guitar and sometimes bass guitar, and Steve played an electric accordion called a Cordovox. All of us sang. This is the first group I was in that had a name, which we took from this scripture.

The Poor of the Flock

And I will feed the flock of slaughter, even you, O poor of the flock. And I took unto Me two staves; the one I called Beauty, and the other I called Bands; and I fed the flock. Zachariah 11:7 (KJV)

No, no! We were not called The Flock of Slaughter. We were called The Poor of the Flock. We were together for a year and a half, ministering at all types of churches and youth groups throughout south central Kansas, and as far away as Kansas City.

With this notoriety and experience in music ministry, I was counting the days until I would be out of the air force so I could launch into music ministry full time. It was God who redirected me, telling me I needed to go to school to learn about what He had called me to do.

"Well, where do You want me to go to school?" I asked the Lord.

"Right here in Wichita."

"Oh," I thought out loud, "so You want me to go to Wichita State University?"

I distinctly and immediately knew in my heart that Wichita State was not the university I was to attend.

"Well, where else is there to go here in Wichita?"

"Friends" was the word God gave me, yet that made no sense to me.

Yet when I looked in the phone book, there it was—Friends University. At that time, I had no

Shamblin solo

9

idea that Friends University was one of the most respected music schools in the world. I only enrolled there because God had told me to do so.

THE FRIENDLY PEOPLE

I left the air force in November 1972 and immediately enrolled at Friends. Once I was registered at the university as a full-time music major, I met a girl named Sharon Evans in the fall of 1973 in music theory class. Sharon introduced me to Collin Featherston, who was also in our class. Collin and Sharon approached me about forming a Christian mixed trio. They had already asked one of the piano majors to play for us.

I told them I would pray about it and agreed to meet with them every Saturday morning to rehearse while waiting on an answer from God. Finally, in January of 1974 the release from God that it was His will for me to be in that group came. After I declared my commitment to Collin and Sharon, that week we received five invitations to sing at five different churches without telling anyone we were available. I booked the first two concerts on the second Sunday in February, and the other three on Friday, Saturday and Sunday evenings of the following weekend. When word got out that we were accepting bookings, every weekend began to fill up, with absolutely no promotion from us of any kind.

At first our repertoire consisted of "cover tunes"—songs that others had written and recorded. This required John, our piano player, to make our musical arrangements work.

On the Tuesday after our first "two-concert Sunday," John informed us that our ministry schedule was much more involved than he had wanted to take on, so he quit the group. We begged him to at least play for the Valentine's banquet coming up in three days, but he was through with us and refused.

Collin and Sharon turned to me after John walked out suggesting we cancel singing for the banquet.

The Friendly People #1

"There is one thing God has taught me that I will not go back on," I declared to them. "Once I have given my word, I will never break it. I will take my guitar and sing at that banquet, even if you are not there with me."

"Well, if you're going, we're going too! What are we going to sing though?"

"I've written a bunch of songs since I got saved," I answered. "I'm going to sing those, and you can harmonize with me."

"Sounds good," Collin responded. "Give me the chords and I can play the songs on guitar with you."

So, without any rehearsal to speak of, the three of us did a full concert that Friday night, playing two guitars and singing three-part harmony.

This was the beginning of the musical group called The Friendly People, a name derived from our university.

The Friendly People #2
L-R: David, Sharon, Debbie, Shamblin, David., Collin

After the Valentine's banquet, we added Debbie Coolie to our group. She was an awesome soprano, and with her we had four-part harmony: Collin sang baritone, I sang tenor, Sharon sang alto, and Debbie sang soprano. Collin played a fretless bass guitar as well as lead acoustic guitar, and I played rhythm guitar on a Guild 12-string. We did all original songs that Sharon or I had written.

By fall of 1974 we had added David Chanowski to the group. David was a music percussion major of the highest caliber at Friends. He played drum kit and vibraphone with us.

David Meineke joined the Friendly People one year later. He was a Wichita State University graduate with a degree in church organ. He was also a good song writer and supplied us with several to sing as a group. By then Debbie had also started writing a few songs for us as well.

MUSIC MINISTRY MIRACLES

Throughout my group and solo music ministries, God taught me and my fellow musicians how to use the power of music to bring people to

Jesus. The greatest miracles I have seen happened when people have come to Christ as a result of my ministry. Here is a story of one of those miracles I learned about many years after the fact.

In 1999, Chris and I and our youngest daughter, Sarah, returned to Wichita after being gone for about thirty years. In 2001, Chris and I were attending the Friends University Symphonic Choir (also known as the Singing Quakers) concert in which Sarah was performing. That's right—Sarah attended my alma mater. We sat down in the only two seats we could find in the large Alumni Auditorium.

While we were waiting for the concert to start, the man next to me leaned over and said, "You're Shamblin Stone."

"That's right. How do you know me?"

After introducing himself as John Martyn, he proceeded to tell me the story of being at a meeting of Asbury Methodist Church youth where I had done a concert. At the end of my concert, I gave an opportunity for people to accept Christ as their Savior. He responded to the altar call that night. Then he told me that he is an ordained pastor in a church near Wichita. I was so thankful that God had those two seats reserved for Chris and me so I would learn of how the fruit from my ministry years ago has remained to this day.

THE PRICE OF MIRACLES

I have experienced many major miracles of all types because I was willing to sacrifice myself to obey God and keep my commitments when I made them. Through doing that I discovered that God honors availability, not ability.

The Friendly People traveled extensively throughout the midwestern and northeastern United States. While at Friends, we averaged three to five concerts per week, sometimes more. Most of the time we would have ministry on Wednesday, Friday, and Saturday nights as well as twice on Sundays. Many times we wouldn't return to Wichita until 2:00 or 3:00 a.m. after ministering twice on Sundays and would have to be in class for eight o'clock on Monday mornings. During the summers our schedule increased because we were touring.

This was our schedule for the three and a half years we were together, but no one complained about it. The rewards from ministering together under the anointing of God far outweighed the sacrifices we made to keep up our schedule.

THE FIRST POWER MIRACLE

Some of the most memorable miracles God did for the Friendly People was giving us power for our amplifiers when there was no natural power available.

The first time this happened was in May 1974 at the Herman Hill Park in Wichita, Kansas. In the seventies, the Herman Hill outdoor stage was the place to be in Wichita, Kansas on a Sunday afternoon for those who enjoyed music. Groups and bands from all over would play there. Nobody knew who would be playing unless the bands advertised themselves, but hundreds of music lovers would show up every Sunday afternoon with their lawn chairs and blankets to enjoy the free concerts.

A young man named Curt had been saved at one of our concerts and was hanging out with me to learn how to book the Friendly People. His dream was one day to become our road manager. As a first assignment, I told Curt to find out for me how music groups scheduled bookings for Sunday afternoons at Herman Hill Park.

Two days later Curt reported back to me that all it took was to buy a permit from the parks and recreation department for five dollars per hour. I threw the bill at him and told him to book us on the first available Sunday afternoon. My plan was not to tell anybody that we were a Christian group until the power in the music had won them over. Then we would present the gospel and appeal to the concert goers to accept Christ as their savior. However, that was my plan—not God's.

Curt booked us for the 2:00 p.m. to 3:00 p.m. slot on the third Sunday of May. I had called a bunch of our Christian friends from different churches where we had played in the past, to let them know we would be singing in the park at that time. I asked if they would come out with their Bibles ready to lead people to the Lord, because I expected a great harvest for Christ that day.

With help we set up the equipment by starting time, excluding a sound check. When I tried to turn on the PA (public address system), the electricity was not on at the stage. We tried all the outlets but none of them worked.

"Curt!" I shouted, and he came running. "Why is there no power?"

"Well, Parks and Recreation said they hire a retired man who lives across the street from the park to come every Sunday and turn the power on and off."

"Well he had better get here fast," I demanded. It was already 2:05 p.m., and the crowd was waiting for some music.

At 2:25 p.m. I saw a group of people pick up their lawn chairs and blanket and leave the park.

"Curt! Go find some way to get this power turned on immediately. I don't want anyone else to leave without having a chance to hear the gospel!"

Curt took off running across the park toward the police sub-station. When I turned around from sending him off, an unfamiliar short, long-haired hippie stood before me.

"Shamblin, call the Christians to prayer!"

"How can I do that? The PA doesn't work."

The hippie leaned toward me, raising himself onto his toes to get closer to my face. "Cup your hands around your mouth!"

Whoever this guy was, he spoke with more authority than I had ever witnessed before, and I knew I had to obey him. Holding my hands to my mouth, I yelled at the top of my lungs, "Any Christians here today, come join me in front of the stage for prayer."

About thirty of us formed a circle where we held hands in front of the stage. Since I was the leader, I felt obligated to pray first. "Oh, God"—I lifted my voice only loud enough for the thirty to hear me—"please help Curt find someone to turn on the power so these hundreds of people can hear the gospel."

The hippie who had commanded me to call for prayer prayed next. He wasn't quiet either. Every person gathered for a concert that day could clearly hear him.

"Lord Jesus," he shouted, "You delivered Joseph from prison, You delivered Your people out of Pharaoh's hands, You delivered David from the mouths of a lion and a bear and from Goliath's hands. Jesus, You delivered Nineveh from Your wrath at Jonah's hands. You delivered Shadrack, Meshach, and Abednego from the fiery furnace, and You delivered Daniel from the lion's den. So, turning on the power here today is no big deal for you!"

Oh, no, I thought. *When this doesn't happen, all these people here today will have another reason to doubt God.*

"So, thank you Jesus," the man went on, "for turning on the power so we can have this concert!"

Noticing some movement in the circle, I looked up to see one of the Christians break out of the circle and climb onto the stage. First, he moved the bass amp so he could plug it into the most forward outlet on stage. Then he brushed his fingers across the bass strings. I had never heard that amp sound that loud before.

Next, he moved the PA forward so it could be plugged into the most forward outlet on the other side of the stage. He reported to me later that God had told him to do that. When he tested a microphone, our system was louder than I had ever heard it before.

Curt had gone to the police station on the other side of the park, where the sergeant told Curt that he usually had to turn on the power every Sunday and would be there soon.

When Curt got back to the stage, we were in the middle of our first song. Bewildered, Curt sat down next to the hippie. "How did we get the power turned on?"

"We prayed," came the response in a matter-of-fact tone.

We were singing our second song by the time the angry policeman arrived. Curt ran to meet him at the side of the stage where the door to the electrical boxes was.

"Why didn't you kids wait?" he shouted at Curt. "I told you I would be right here! Why did you have to break in and turn on the power?"

"We didn't break in," Curt responded. "Check the padlock and the door. It's still locked and there's no sign of forced entry."

After closely examining the lock and door, the officer turned to Curt. "Then how did you get the power turned on?"

"They said," Curt answered slowly, "that they prayed."

The policeman then staggered in front of the stage to some stumps where he sat down in the shade. Curt stayed close by him but did not interrupt his thoughts. After we had done a couple more songs, the officer walked back in front of the stage to the door where the electrical panels were at stage left. Curt followed him.

This time the officer opened the door and crawled under the stage. After a few minutes he emerged and locked the door with the padlock.

"I don't know where you kids are getting your power from," the officer told Curt, "because there is nothing turned on under there. I guess I'll come back in an hour . . ." He caught himself. "Wait a minute. I can't come back and turn off the power. I didn't turn it on. Well, play as long as you want, I guess!" The officer walked back to the sub-station still shaking his head.

Later we checked with almost all the Christians—no one had ever seen that hippie before, and he's never been seen since that day. Some have suggested, especially since he knew my name, that he was an angel. I believe them.

MORE POWER MIRACLES

In all, God turned on the power supernaturally five times while the Friendly People were ministering together. That had never happened for any of us before we formed the group, and neither has it happened to any of us as individuals since the group has broken up. Here are two more of those miracles.

We were providing the music for a Full Gospel Businessman's Fellowship International chapter meeting in New York state when another power miracle occurred. After the speaker gave his testimony, he asked us to come back up and lead in some soft worship while he prayed for people. We were singing a third song when Collin, our bass player, began to shout, "Who! I can't believe it! Hallelujah!"

Since the girls were carrying the song vocally, and I could walk around and play my guitar, I went over to him and asked, "What's going on?"

"I forgot," he said, hyperventilating, "to turn on the bass amp after we came back up here!"

He pointed to the amp. When I looked, the red power light was not on ". . . and I've played the last three songs with the power off," Collin finished.

That kicked up the meeting a few spiritual levels. We saw major verifiable healings take place that night as a result of the increase in faith that occurred from that supernatural power miracle.

Another miracle occurred at a Christian coffeehouse in New York state. They had heard that we were in their area, so they asked us to come over on a Friday night to perform an outreach concert in the town park. The coffeehouse had blanketed the town with posters advertising the concert in the park.

We got to town with just barely enough time to handle the two-hour setup for the concert. We placed ourselves in the grass next to the large pavilion because there was a streetlight by the pavilion that would illuminate the park at night. The pavilion itself had only power outlets but no light fixtures.

We were just finishing the setup and getting ready to do our sound check when the town policeman drove into the park. After he introduced himself to me, he asked, "Why are you setting up for a concert here in the park with all this sound gear?"

The coffeehouse director jumped into the conversation. "Well, I got a permit from your office."

"I know that," the officer explained. "But we didn't know when we issued the permit that you would need power for your amplifiers!"

"Well, there's power outlets in this pavilion," the director explained. "That's where we were going to plug into, if that's all right?"

"You can plug into them if you like, but there's no power in the outlets," the officer explained.

"Well, sure there is!" the director rebutted. "This streetlight is lighting up the whole park, so there's power here in the park, isn't there?"

"There is power to the streetlight," the officer patiently explained, "but the power cable has been removed from the streetlight to the pavilion. Take a look," he insisted. "Do you see a cable running from the streetlight pole to the pavilion? No, you don't because the town council voted last year to remove it. Now do you understand what I am telling you?"

While this conversation was going on, the people from the town had already begun to gather with their lawn chairs.

"Should we go back to the coffeehouse to do the concert?" the director asked me.

"We're looking at another two-hours plus to set up again. I don't think the people will wait that long. Do you?"

"No." He shook his head. "What are we going to do?"

"Lord," I prayed under my breath, "please help us to minister to these people."

"Go plug your extension cord into the farthest outlet away from you," the Lord said to my spirit.

To do that I had to move the amps back about five feet. Once that was done and I'd plugged the extension cord in where God told me, I yelled to David to turn on the PA. He did and the blue light came on indicating there was power to the amp.

"Test a mic," I yelled again.

"Test, test, one, two, three," David's voice boomed throughout the park from our speakers.

All the amps worked that night plugged into an outlet that wasn't connected to any source of natural power. The town constable confirmed that we experienced a verifiable miracle that evening.

HERMAN HILL PARK FOLLOW-UP #1

When God does special miracles like this, it's easy to get proud and think we are better than others who are doing what we're doing. I am sorry to say that for almost a year after that Herman Hill Park miracle we felt special and (just speaking for myself) puffed up with pride. After all, we were not hearing about any other Christian music groups that God was turning on the power for.

Leading up to that concert in Herman Hill Park, I had felt that event would be significant to the Kingdom of God, an evangelistic harvest of souls that day of Billy Graham proportions. However, when I made the appeal for people to come to Christ, not one person out of hundreds accepted my challenge to become a Christian, even after witnessing that major power miracle.

I couldn't understand why God did such a miracle while knowing there would be no fruit from His efforts. That thought opened me to the lies of the enemy. Satan told me that the reason God did that miracle in Herman Hill Park was to show everybody how special we were. Thank God He did not leave us in that deception for a long time. Rather, He had mercy on us and let us know the real reason for his actions that day in Herman Hill Park.

Almost a year after the Herman Hill power miracle, the Friendly

People were booked for a five-night revival at the Wesley United Methodist Church (WUMC) in Wichita, Kansas. The pastor of the WUMC placed posters with our picture on them in businesses near the church.

Each evening we as a group sang for about thirty minutes, then I preached an evangelistic message, followed by an appeal for people to receive Jesus as their Lord and Savior.

On the Friday evening of that week at WUMC five people respond to the altar call for salvation: a man, a woman, and three children between the ages of eight and twelve. I prayed with the man, Debbie (our soprano) prayed with the woman, and the pastor of the church got to led the three children to the Lord.

As we were leaving the church that evening, the pastor said to me, "You know, those children, they are your fruit."

"What do you mean?" I asked as he was turning out the lights. "Aren't they part of a family who attends your church?"

"No. I've never seen them before tonight."

"Well," I was puzzled, "where did they come from?"

"They said they live in the neighborhood," the pastor explained. "They told me a story I didn't really understand. They said they heard you sing last summer in Herman Hill Park. Something about God turning on the power that day. They said they'd been looking for you ever since that happened, to give their lives to Christ, because they were too embarrassed that day to respond."

They had also told the pastor how they saw our poster in the QuickTrip convenience store across the street from the church and knew they had to show up that night.

"As far as I can figure out," the pastor concluded, "those kids came here tonight with their minds already made up that they were going to get saved. They were just waiting for you to ask."

"Wow, so that's why God turned on the power that day. It was for them, not us." My eyes began to tear up as I realized what had happened and explained it to the pastor.

We didn't see the kids on Saturday evening, but on Sunday evening they came back and brought their older teenage brother and mother. When it was time for the altar call, both gave their lives to Jesus.

THE MUSIC FESTIVAL OF JOY

After that series of revival meetings in April, the Friendly People hosted the first Jesus Music Festival of Joy in May of that year at Joyland Amusement Park in Wichita, Kansas. Of course, that month was also the end of the school year, which meant extra events, school concerts, and finals.

I had negotiated a deal with the park owner, Stan Nelson, to charge one gate price on the two days of the festival, which would allow the attendees to ride all the rides as many times as they wanted and also attend all the eleven hours per day of Christian music concerts.

The Jesus Musical Festival of Joy (FOJ) became an annual event for four years. Held on the Saturday and Sunday of Memorial Day weekend each year, twenty or more local, regional, and nationally known Christian musicians and ministries performed and ministered at the park.

Collin   David C.   Debbie   Sharon   Shamblin   Dave M.
The Friendly People at the Jesus Music Festival of Joy, 1976

Gary Smith, an architect/engineer friend, had designed and built the permanent stage especially for the festival. The week before the 1975 FOJ he had the leaders of the festival pray over the stage to dedicate it to the glory of God. He also placed a plaque on the stage that declared the date we dedicated this stage to the Lord Jesus Christ. Gary had researched the entire back lot of Joyland Amusement Park to determine the best place to put the stage. He designed it to face an old creek bed since he had been told no water had filled the space for at least twenty-five years.

To make this event work, we recruited about 50 to 60 volunteers from the various Christian denominations we had ministered to. It was one of the largest displays of Christian unity Wichita had seen up to that point.

1975 was our maiden voyage for the "Music Festival of Joy." We hosted the event for three years (1975, 1976, and 1977), then turned it over to Tony Napier, the Director of the Wichita area Youth for Christ to continue the event since the Friendly People had disbanded, I had graduated from university, and had moved out of Wichita.

Tony Napier at the FOJ

Tony only got to do the FOJ on the Memorial Day weekend of 1978, because in October of that year he was driving behind a plumber's truck on McLean Boulevard, and one of the pipes on that truck came loose and broke through his windshield. He went to be with Jesus that day. After that, no one picked up the mantle of the FOJ, so that was its last year.

Shamblin and Tony at the FOJ

That first year of the FOJ we had a low budget consisting only of offerings the Friendly People had received from concerts to promote with. The only way we could give our out-of-town music groups and ministering guests any money to cover their expenses was to wait for the gate receipts to be counted, which we were splitting with Joyland Amusement Park.

Even with a low promotional budget that first year, we had more than 7,000 attend the festival, which was well beyond our expectations. Knowing God wanted the FOJ to be an annual event, I started a special bank account with the proceeds we received from splitting the gate with Joyland. That money was to only be used to promote next year's festival.

Our keynote speaker in 1975 was Mike Warnke. He had published a book called *The Satan Seller* a couple of years previously. It was his testimony of being converted from a satanic high priest to serving Jesus.

Mike spoke four times during the two days of the festival. He preached a wonderful evangelistic sermon on the Saturday night and gave an altar call where several people responded to receive Christ as their Savior. Then Mike taught a Sunday school lesson on Sunday morning, and we had a Sunday morning service for the campers and others who were there from out of town. The final time Mike spoke was the finale of the event on Sunday evening.

Mike Warnke at the FOJ talking to Pat Spear, the chief stage manager

Saturday night and Sunday morning it had rained hard. The ground was saturated in Joyland's back lot, and the old creek bed in front of the stage had about eight inches of standing water in it. To get closer to the stage, many people carried picnic tables from the nearby pavilions to sit on. No one could put tables directly in front of the stage, however, due to the standing water. Even though the sun was out all day, the area right in front of the stage still had six inches of standing water when the sun set Sunday evening.

It was clear to me from listening to Mike preach and teach the Bible how much he loved the Word of God and that he was functioning in his calling. He knew he was doing what God had called him to do, so he was reluctant to share his testimony that Sunday night.

"I don't want to look back," Mike told me that Sunday afternoon in a private conversation. "I want to focus on who I am in Christ today!"

"I understand that. But the people who will be here tonight are expecting to hear your testimony. That's what I advertised you'll be sharing."

"Well," Mike said as he sighed, "I'll pray about it."

I wasn't sure what Mike was going to share that night, even up to the point when he was being introduced.

Frank Edmonson was our emcee for the FOJ all four years. He had attended Friends University, gone on to have a weekly, nationally syndicated "Jesus Music" radio show, and was the director of Mhyrr Records (the contemporary Christian music division of Word Records out of Waco, Texas).

From the stage at night all that could be seen was the two 1500-watt flood lights washing everything away before him. The only way we knew there were people out there was by the applause and verbal sounds they made. For someone like Mike, who was used to reading the faces of his audiences as he spoke, that night was torturous.

Because of this, while Mike was speaking, I positioned myself standing on the ground behind the speakers at stage right so he could see my face. Whatever he was going to speak about, I wanted to provide him with as much support as I could regardless of his chosen topic.

"I know many of you came here tonight to hear me give my testimony," Mike began, "but I don't do that anymore. It gives too much attention to the devil, and I want to lift up Jesus!"

The FOJ Emcee Frank Edmonson, known as Paul Baker to his radio audience

I think Mike expected some sort of audible validation from the audience like cheers or applause at that statement, but it never came. The silence visibly shook Mike, and he glanced nervously around the stage floor trying to decide what to do

"Well, I'll give a little bit of my testimony," Mike back-peddled, "before I get into the Word."

The crowd erupted with cheers and applause. For the next hour and a half Mike shared his story of conversion from being sold out to Satan to being sold out to Jesus. The crowd was riveted to every word he said and would have sat there longer if Mike kept talking. The Holy Spirit was upon Mike, which kept the crowd hanging on his every word. Likewise, the Holy Spirit knew exactly when to lead Mike to ask people to make the same commitment he had made—to give their lives to Christ.

"If the Spirit of God is drawing you to Jesus tonight," Mike concluded, I want you to come and stand right here in front of this stage with me, and we're going to pray together for you to receive Christ as your Savior!"

The FOJ stage on Sunday 1975, showing how close the crowds could get the picnic tables to the front of the stage, and the area they had to avoid because of the standing water. The name of the group performing here is unknown.

As people came forward in the dark to give their lives to Jesus, we could hear the sloshing of many feet in the water in front of the stage. Mike turned to me in panic then shrugged his shoulders and held out the mic to me. I jumped onto the stage and took it from him. He then sat down and slid off the stage, landing in the water to be with dozens of those ready for their new lives. As I leaned over from the stage, holding the mic for him so he wouldn't get electrocuted, Mike Warnke led those people to Jesus!

FOLLOW-UP ABOUT MIKE WARNKE

Frank called me in the Fall that year and told me he had signed Mike Warnke to a recording contract with his record label. His first record was his testimony, and many more albums followed. Mike filled large venues everywhere he went to speak until a Chicago Christian magazine tried to destroy his ministry by accusing him of not being truthful in his stories. In my opinion, the magazine took everything Mike said literally despite that it was clear that his style of comedy thrived on hyperbole.

Satan used that magazine to falsely accuse Mike, and no one came to his defense except for a few close friends. I have often wondered how many more people would have made it to heaven because of Mike's ministry if that magazine had handled their grievance with him according to Scripture instead of using the world's method of destroying Mike's reputation. I speculate that the number of Mike's converts would have rivaled Billy

Graham's numbers by now if he had been allowed to complete his mission unhindered. Mike is still preaching the Word today by God's grace, but that magazine hasn't been heard from for several years. God still gets the last word.

HERMAN HILL PARK FOLLOW-UP #2

A week and a half after the Festival of Joy, the Friendly People started our summer-long tour.

Summer tour 1975 of the Friendly People in a 1974 VW bus: We carried a PA with monitors, 6 mics on stands, two guitars, a bass guitar and amp, a full set of drums, and six people inside. Our luggage went on the roof rack.

For about three weeks of those three months we were touring our keyboard player toured with us, making it seven people in a five-passenger van.

By June we had made it as far as Des Moines, Iowa. We had concerts and services scheduled from Sunday to Sunday there, with only the Monday off. Our hosts for the week had a huge house, with room for all six of us, which made it nice for us to all be under one roof.

On Saturday, Collin received a letter from his girlfriend, who was in Wichita. Shortly after receiving the letter, Collin told me he had something to share with the group, so we gathered at the dining room table.

Collin began reading the letter. "Do you remember the three kids? The ones who were at Herman Hill Park when God turned on the power for you. The ones who got saved in April at the Wesley United Methodist Church." We all nodded to each other. "Well, they lived on a cul-de-sac with a neighbor who had a pickup truck. Every Saturday the neighbor put all the kids in the back of his pickup and took them to the little league baseball games. Last Saturday, on their way home from the games, the pickup truck died on the railroad tracks. A train struck the truck . . . and they died."

Everyone at the table began to weep. The reality of just how much the Lord loves those three children hit me hard. He knew their time to die was coming soon, so He brought those kids to Herman Hill Park to observe a power miracle started by a prayer of faith. God then moved on the pastor of the church in their neighborhood to invite us for an event and prompted him to put up posters with the Friendly People's picture on it. And then He directed the kids to get drinks at the QuickTrip where they saw our poster. God did all this just to give those children a chance at salvation before they would die.

THE PROPHETIC PRINCIPLE

After the week in Des Moines, we spent a week in Waterloo, Iowa hosted by a Christian music group who had been at the Festival of Joy with us in May. It was in Waterloo that God warned us about what was to happen in just two short months on that tour.

We were booked every evening that week in different churches in the area. During the days we either got together for Bible study, practice, or songwriting, or we just hung out in the homes where we were staying because our hosts had day jobs.

On Friday the host group's leader came home from work shaken and stopped our preparations for that evening to talk to us.

"I was standing at my drill press today," he began, "when the Lord told me something was about to happen to you guys that will test your collective faith more than you could ever imagine."

We all glanced at each other to see how the others reacted to this. David finally broke the silence. "Well, what is it?"

"I don't know," he answered. "All I know is that it will be bad—really bad."

I didn't know or understand the Word of God then like I do now. Throughout the years God has revealed an important promise He made to His people: He will always tell us before anything happens to us, good or bad. I have come to understand this promise as the prophetic principle, which is summarized for us in this scripture:

> *Surely the Lord God does nothing, Unless He reveals His secret to His servants the prophets. Amos 3:7 (NKJV)*

Here is another scripture referring to this principle.

> *Behold, the former things are come to pass, and new things do I **declare**: before they spring forth **I tell you** of them. Isaiah 42:9 (KJV) emphasis added*

God will ALWAYS tell us before something happens that it is going to happen so we know for sure that God is in control no matter the outcome. Here is a verse which tells us that.

> *I have even from the beginning **declared** it to thee; before it came to pass I **shewed** it thee: lest thou shouldest say, Mine idol hath done them, and my graven image, and my molten image, hath commanded them. Isaiah 48:5 (KJV) emphasis added*

Only God can make sure we know about something before it happens, then bring it to pass. No human, and no devil can do that! This is God's prophetic principle, and it's how He operates ALL the time.

You may ask how God tells us things if we don't know how to hear or recognize His voice. Remember I told you in the book *Portrait of a Worshiper* that the more time we spend in the Word of God, the more we will learn to recognize God's voice?

It really does not depend on our ability to hear God speak. We will hear Him even if we don't believe He speaks to us.[1] God talks to you all the time. It is our job to learn to recognize when He is talking to us. If we have not yet learned how to recognize His voice, God has a backup plan for getting His messages to us: prophesy. Prophesy means to speak as God's mouthpiece.

> *If any man speak, let him speak as the oracles of God; if any man minister, let him do it as of the ability which God giveth: that God in all things may be glorified through Jesus Christ, to whom be praise and dominion for ever and ever. Amen. 1 Peter 4:11 (KJV)*

God never intended for just a select few to be able to hear from Him and speak on his behalf. God wants everyone of us to be able to hear His voice and prophesy to those around us so His message will be clearly heard. This instance with Moses reveals to us God's heart regarding who He wants to prophesy.

> *And there ran a young man, and told Moses, and said, Eldad and Medad do prophesy in the camp. And Joshua the son of Nun, the servant of Moses, one of his young men, answered and said, My lord Moses, forbid them. And Moses said unto him, Enviest thou for my sake? would God that all the Lord's people were prophets, and that the Lord would put His spirit upon them! Numbers 11:27-29 (KJV)*

We are also told that prophesy will increase the closer we get to Christ's return.

> *And it shall come to pass **in the last days**, saith God, I will pour out of My Spirit upon all flesh: and your sons and your daughters shall **prophesy**, and your young men shall see visions, and your old men shall dream dreams: And on My servants and on My handmaidens I will pour out in those*

---

[1] John 10:27

*days of My Spirit; and they shall **prophesy**: Acts 2:17-18 (KJV) emphasis added*

Don't think that the people who know how to hear the voice of God will be the only ones prophesying. God has ways of speaking through people even when they don't know He is doing so.

Have you ever been talking to someone when something they said seemed so significant you wouldn't ignore it, and later you realized God was talking to you through them? God will even use a non-Christian like this. After all, he did use a donkey as His mouthpiece[2] because Balaam, a prophet, was not listening to Him.

So, how does this work?

A lion has roared! Who will not fear? The Lord God has spoken! Who can but prophesy? Amos 3:8 (NKJV)

Let's say you and I planned an outing to the zoo together. While we are leisurely walking around the grounds, we notice everyone running for the main gate, and the zookeeper pulls up to us in his golf cart.

"Please, do not panic," he begins, "but the lions have all escaped their enclosure, and I need everyone to move as quickly as possible to the main gate and leave the zoo!"

"How did this happen?" I questioned.

"They mauled one of my staff at feeding time," he shouted over his shoulder as he drove away.

You and I look at each other then turn at the same time toward the direction of the main gate. As we turn, we hear a loud roaring lion as close as ten yards away. Do you think we would have been able to keep from being afraid at that moment? *"A lion has roared! Who will not fear?"*

In the same way, if God wants to speak through you, you will prophesy whether you know what you are doing or not. *"The Lord God has spoken! Who can but prophesy?"*

---

[2] Numbers 22:22-35

APPROACHING THE END OF SUMMER TOUR 1975

We started on our way back across the country toward Wichita. Our schedule would put us in Wichita just a couple of days before the Fall semester at Friends University began.

We had ministered an average of six times a week on that summer tour. Many places where we sang gave us "love offerings" for our ministry, but the expenses of traveling and keeping six people fed for two and a half months had exhausted that income. To get us home, I had borrowed money from the Festival of Joy account I had set up earlier that summer.

It took two weeks for God to convince me to withdraw some of that money to get us home. I only did it with a solemn promise to God that we would repay that money with future offerings as soon as possible. The memory of hearing those people walking in the water to receive Christ made that money more important to me than life itself. It was meant to be the difference between life and death for the people who would give their lives to Christ the following year at the FOJ, and these were people I hadn't even met yet.

As the fourth of August approached, the Friendly People had been on tour for a little more than two months. Since nothing bad had happened all summer, we'd forgotten about God's warning back in Waterloo, Iowa. There was probably a symbolic reason why God chose that town to give us the warning in—we were about to meet our waterloo. But I don't want to read too much into it.

We had ministered twice that Sunday in the same church in a town located in southern Pennsylvania, just sixty-five miles north of Washington D.C. Our next ministry time wasn't until Tuesday evening, and since we had off Monday, the pastor's wife suggested we stay with them one more night and spend the day seeing Washington D.C sights. None of us had ever been there before, so we accepted her offer.

We drove down early to D.C. on Monday and stayed busy sightseeing all day. The last place we went was the Smithsonian Institute. Our tour guide told us that there were enough exhibits across the Smithsonian museums that, if we spent two minutes at each exhibit, it would take twelve years without sleep to see everything.

The museum was open late that evening, so four hours went by before we realized we were late leaving the city according to the time we told our hosts we would be back. It took us quite a while to walk back to our VW bus from the museum given the vastness of the Smithsonian's campus.

By the time we returned to where we had parked our van, it was around 10:00 p.m. A mist hung in the air, so I rolled down my window to see the street signs as we navigated out of D.C toward the Beltway. The closer we made it to the highway that would lead us to Pennsylvania, we realized that we were all starving. By that time, it was after 11:00 p.m.

Thank goodness we soon came across a McDonald's. The golden arches danced for us as we parked and went inside to order.

The dine-in area was closed, so the two armed guards dressed in security uniforms and utility belts filled with hand cuffs, night sticks, and the same type of hand gun I had carried when I was a security policeman in the air force caught my attention in the otherwise empty building.

THE FULFILMENT OF PROPHESY

We got our orders from the MickeyD's counter and headed back to the van. Collin was always the servant, so he was carrying the bags of food and the trays of drinks for all of us, so everyone just went on ahead and got in the van.

Being from the Midwest in the 1970s, I was functioning with that mentality regarding our security, so I had left my window down while we had gone into the restaurant. Once I had gotten back into the driver's seat, while watching over my right shoulder for Collin, I realized the mist had disappeared, so I turned to roll up my window then shifted my attention back toward the side door as I cranked the window up. Part way through this, I heard a bump, but I chose not to check it out until I had my Big Mac in my hand.

Everyone was in the van except for Collin, who was standing at the side door, his eyes as big as saucers. Beside Collin stood a teenager with a gun pointed in his direction.

Seeing that, I quickly turned back toward my door to see another kid yelling at me. I had caught the barrel of his gun and had rolled it up in my window, leaving him with only my wife Chris to shoot. Not wanting her to get shot, I rolled down my window halfway so he would point the gun at me instead.

"You got any money?" I could now hear him screaming at me. "Give me your money!"

My mind raced. Did I have any money? Well, not me personally. The money I did have in my wallet belonged to God. It was the money from the Festival of Joy account, and I didn't have permission from God to do anything with that money but get us home. Therefore, I had purposed that I would die before I let anything happen to that money. It was not my money; it was God's.

This thought process took a couple of minutes—time in which I did not respond to the robber outside my van door. When I put my mind back on the situation at hand, he was clenching his teeth and raising his voice at me for my lack of response to his continued demands for money.

I then heard a voice from the back of our van say, "Tell him to get out of the car!"

"Get out of the car!" The robber stomped his foot.

That is what I had wanted all along. Before I was drafted and joined the air force, I was a serious student of Shotokan karate. I'd even taken classes on how to disarm someone with a handgun, and I knew what to do when I was standing face-to-face with someone with a gun. While I had been considering my current situation, though, I hadn't been able to figure out how to exit the vehicle without tipping off the robber. When he told me to get out of the van, I knew God had delivered him into my hand.

The first rule when preparing to disarm someone is never to let them get more than an arm's length away from you. Within an arm's length away, it's possible to grab their gun hand in one quick movement. A distance that requires stepping before grabbing, however, is two movements that gives them enough time to pull the trigger.

When I left my vehicle, I stepped within an arm's length of my robber. My closeness made him uncomfortable, so he took a step backward, to which I stepped forward to maintain my arm's length from him. Shouted demands for money matched his continual backward movements as I pursued him all the way to where his buddy was at the rear of our van. When they got side-by-side, they glanced at each other, said, "Let's get out of here!" and ran as fast as they could toward the trees behind the restaurant.

The third kid who had collected the wallets and purses from the other band members had arrived at the back of the van in time to hear and see his cohorts run away.

"No, wait!" he shouted after them.

They didn't slow down. They didn't even turn around.

This young seventeen-year-old boy turned to me and said, "You got any money?"

Since I had already processed the answer to that question, I didn't have to think about my answer when asked the second time.

"NO!"

He flinched and because he had the gun cocked, it went off at point-blank range. To keep myself from falling to the ground, I fell toward the side of the van and held myself up. When I didn't go down, the boy ran off in the direction of his friends.

From the passenger seat, Chris saw me get shot through the side windows of the van. She also saw the two armed guards positioned near the front door of the restaurant as they watched the robbery and shooting take place. Yet they never came out to help, even after the robbers were gone.

I started to panic. But as I leaned against that van, God said, "It's all right!" I'm not sure if His voice was audible or just in my spirit, but the words filtered the panic out of me.

I went into "war-zone" mentality, and grabbed my van keys from my pocket as I climbed into the driver's seat. I then started the car. All I could think about was how I had to get my squad to safety before I could assess my own injuries.

As I was doing this, Chris asked me, "Are you OK?"

"No." I put the van in reverse.

When I turned to look over my shoulder to back out of the parking place, severe pain radiated through me and everything went black. The clutch popped, which killed the engine, and the van stalled in the middle of the parking lot.

I was sinking into a black hole, and the light outside the hole got further and further away. I fought as hard as I could to climb out of that hole, to get to the light. Chris told me later that at that time I looked like I was trying to claw my way through the windshield. This went on for a couple of minutes until Chris grabbed my shoulders and shook me.

"SHAMBLIN!" she yelled.

With that I was no longer in the hole but rather I was back in the driver's seat of our van and in extreme pain. I had never felt that much pain before nor have I since! I also felt the heat of the bullet in my body.

David jumped out of the van and ran around to the driver's door. He and Chris laid me down across the front seats of the van. My head hung off the passenger seat in such a way that I was looking at everything upside down.

"We need help here!" David yelled at the door of the restaurant.

By this time their entire staff had joined the security guards at the door, but no one came to see what they could do to help.

Frustrated by their lack of help, David screamed, "Can somebody at least call an ambulance?"

None of them budged. After a couple of minutes, the night manager went inside and called the police. Still no one from that restaurant ever set foot outside the building to help us.

It took about ten minutes for the police to get there. I saw them upside down pull into the parking lot with lights and sirens going.

"Has anyone called an ambulance yet?" the policeman yelled as he exited his car.

"No!" David yelled back at him.

The policeman climbed into his car. "I'll call them," he shouted before sitting down.

It took another ten minutes for the ambulance to arrive with its sirens and lights screaming.

In an effort to keep from laying directly on my back, I had raised my head and was holding onto the steering wheel with my right hand. A VW van is narrow enough to do that. The paramedics had to pry my hand from the steering wheel to slide me onto the gurney

Once in the ambulance, I held myself up by holding onto the side rail of the gurney. That didn't help much because the ride was so bumpy, causing me unbearable pain.

We arrived at the ambulance bay of Washington D.C. General Hospital about thirty-five minutes after I was shot, and I was rushed inside. Once they transferred me to the ER bed, I was surrounded by nurses and doctors. Someone was at my right arm putting in an IV line, two nurses went to work removing my clothes, and another was at my left side getting my vitals. An ER doctor was talking to the paramedics.

The nurse on my left put the blood pressure cuff on my left arm and began pumping it up. *Shhhhhhh* came the sound of the air escaping from the cuff.

"Oh, my God." The nurse gasped. "He doesn't have any blood pressure!"

Upon hearing that, the ER doctor pushed the two nurses out of the way, grabbed his stethoscope, and proceeded to pump up the cuff himself. *Shhhhhhh* . . .

"Oh, my God, you're right." He ran out of the room to call a surgeon.

When I heard that, I started to panic again. *You've got to have some blood pressure to be alive, don't you?* My mind was racing from one thought to another. *I may see Jesus tonight.*

At that moment I heard the same three words that I had heard from God right after I was shot. "It's all right!"

"That's easy for you to say," I said to the Lord. *"You're not the one who has been shot!"*

The peace of God's presence overwhelmed me, and I knew that, no matter what I had to go through, I would not die because God had told me twice it would be all right. With that realization, I completely relaxed.

"I'll probably have to go through surgery, and a recovery time," I told myself, "but at least I will not die." That much was settled!

WAITING FOR SURGERY

Once every stitch of my clothing was off, one of the nurses started shaving my chest and belly in preparation for surgery. Another nurse was working on putting in a catheter when a candy striper came in with a clipboard and pen.

"Mr. Stone"—she leaned over my face—"would you please sign this release form so we can operate on you?"

"Why can't you have my wife sign it?" I responded.

"Well," she answered, "the police took your wife downtown to question her about the shooting. . . ."

Frustrated to find out that Chris wasn't even at the hospital with me, I signed the form as she held the clipboard above my face.

Next, someone came in with a portable x-ray machine to get a chest x-ray. The bullet needed to be located since there was no exit wound.

Finally, the preparations for surgery were done, so they covered me with a sheet, as if I had any dignity left. The surgeon kept checking on me every fifteen minutes or so. Once I heard him discussing with my ER nurse his disappoint over having to wait on an operating room for me.

"They told me all the operating rooms are full," she answered him, "and they will call as soon as one becomes available."

"Well, that better be soon!," the surgeon snapped back at her. "This guy doesn't have much time!"

So, there I lay in the ER, alone, waiting, wondering, and believing that I would die an old man but not that day. The nurse and surgeon continued to check on me every few minutes.

About two and a half hours after I had arrived at the hospital, the candy striper came back into my room with a clipboard and pen.

"Mr. Stone," she got in my face once again, "could you sign this form for me so we can operate on you?"

"I already signed it." My speech was slurred as I responded to her. "Why do you want me to sign it again?"

"Well," she hesitated, "I lost the first one."

This time when I signed, I barely had the strength to hold up the pen, and my signature was just a squiggly line that trailed off the page.

Toward the end of my wait for surgery, I started to drift off to sleep. I was jolted back into consciousness when the surgeon started pushing my bed out of the ER room as he shouted instructions to the ER nurse.

"Call surgery and tell them I'm on my way. I don't care if I have to operate in the hall. I can't wait any longer!"

I watched the hallway ceiling zoom by as he ran toward the elevator. It was an old building, and the elevator floor was slightly higher than the hallway floor, which gave me a jolt of extreme pain going on and off the elevator.

When the elevator door opened, I looked between my feet and saw a nurse sitting at the desk. After we cleared the elevator door, he turned my feet to the right, where I saw an empty and ready operating room

"Why didn't someone call and tell us this room was available?" The surgeon raised his voice at the nurse as he hurried me into the room. "I've been waiting more than three hours to operate on this patient!"

"Oh, Doctor," the nurse responded, "you mean no one called? That room's been available for an hour and a half."

WATCHING MY SURGERY

They moved me onto the operating table, which was extremely painful, and put the mask over my nose and mouth. I took three breaths and was suddenly no longer in pain. However, I was also no longer inside my body but near the ceiling of the operating room looking down upon myself being operated on. I did not go anywhere else during my out-of-body experience. God had told me it would be all right, so I simply wanted to stay close for the fulfillment of that promise.

The surgeon grabbed a scalpel as soon as he got to the table and made a deep cut from just below my sternum toward my waist. As he was cutting, he realized he was headed toward my naval, so he curved his cut around it, then stopped cutting about three inches below my naval. I have had a couple of doctors tell me over the years that the incision he made was what doctors do when performing an autopsy, which indicated to them that he did not expect me to live.

The robbers used handguns called "Saturday night specials," .22 caliber tumble action guns, which meant the bullet the robber used on me didn't rifle (spin). Once the bullet met with resistance—my body—it tumbled unpredictably, doing potentially more damage at close range than a rifling bullet. I was shot at "point-blank" range, not more than three feet away, and the bullet entered my chest just under my heart.

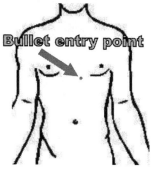

Once it struck my body, the bullet tumbled down, destroying about a third of my liver where the vena cava runs through it. The bullet also clipped the vena cava, nearly severing it. The vena cava is the largest vein in the body, and it carries blood back to the heart. Where it passes through the liver, it is slightly smaller than the diameter of a man's thumb.

The X-rays had revealed that the bullet was about two inches to the right of my spine, a couple of inches below my right shoulder blade, and about two inches inside my back muscle. Keep in mind that the weapon used to shoot me was a tumble action barrel, not a rifle action. A bullet shot from a rifling gun barrel is spinning as well as being projected forward. This makes the bullet travel in the straight line, and bore through whatever it comes in contact with. A tumble action gun will cause the bullet too act in unpredictable ways, bouncing around in the body. The position where the bullet came to rest explained why it hurt so bad to lay on my back. The surgeon had determined that the bullet would not cause any more damage where it was, so he announced to the ones in the OR that he would not be going after it.

As my spirit hovered above the table while the doctor performed the surgery, memories of cowboy duels came to mind. Growing up in the era I did, I watched an overabundance of cowboy shows such as *Roy Rogers, The Lone Ranger, Maverick,* and *Gunsmoke.* Shooting happened regularly in these Westerns, and if by chance someone got shot and didn't die, the most urgent thing the doctor always did was dig the bullet out of the wounded person's body to save them from lead poisoning.

I didn't then and still don't now understand enough about medicine to follow the surgeon's activities during the operation. I just remember being frustrated with his apparent lack of plans to take the bullet out of my body because of my cowboy shows indoctrination.

He, on the other hand, was most concerned with fixing the vein, which was only connected by a thin piece of tissue. After working on it for a couple of hours, he sighed in relief. There was nothing he could do to repair the liver. If I lived, the liver would heal and regenerate, he reasoned.

To close me up, since he had made such a large incision, he first used six large retention sutures, which drew and held all the layers of tissue and muscle together. These reminded me of clothesline rope. Next, he wired the layers of muscle together, then sutured the skin together.

With that he announced he had done all he could do to save my life and instructed the nurses to take me to the surgical intensive care unit. His plan was to check on me in a few hours to see if I had survived.

AFTER SURGERY

I followed my body through the halls and into an open ward, separated only by hanging curtains. My bed was the closest to the corner nurse's station, and they left the curtain open so they could keep an eye on me. My body simply appeared to me to be sleeping.

I do not know how much time went by before the surgeon came in dressed in a shirt and tie and lab coat. I assume he went home and slept a few hours before coming in to see me. He appeared freshly showered and rested since I had seen him after the three hours of intense surgery preceded by the three-hour wait for surgery.

He told the nurse standing nearby that he wanted to try to get me off the breathing machine so I would not become dependent on it if I survived. With that he and three nurses took a few steps to my bedside, where he began to shake me to wake me up.

At that moment I realized it was time to re-enter my body so I could communicate with the doctor. When I did, I felt indescribable pain once again, as I looked at the doctor through my body's eyes.

"We want to turn off this breathing machine," he explained to me, "but you will have to breathe on your own when we do. Do you think you can do that?"

I was still trying to reorient myself, and deal with the overwhelming pain. Besides, my mouth was taped shut with all types of tubes coming out of everywhere. I tried to talk but couldn't. I also had no idea if I could breathe on my own. I had just gotten back inside my body, for goodness sake!

The doctor was on the right side of my bed, and the breathing machine was on the left side up near my head. He motioned for the nurse nearest the machine to flip off the switch and waited intently to see if I would breath on my own. I did not. The last thing I remember before blacking out was three nurses and a doctor diving toward the machine to turn it back on.

After a moment I caught my breath and looked up at four sets of wide eyes staring at me to make sure I was breathing.

"I'll come back in a while," the doctor told the nurses, "and we'll try this again. If we don't get him off this breathing machine, he'll be on it for the rest of his life."

They dispersed from my bed, and I drifted off to sleep. I never left my body after that, so a couple of hours later I woke up to find the surgeon shaking me once more.

"We're going to try this again," he said to me. "I need you to really try to breathe on your own!"

That time I nodded to him, so he knew I understood his words.

"Lord Jesus," I prayed silently. "You breathed breath into Adam's nostrils when you created him. Please breathe breath into me now!

The surgeon took no chance this time. He stood beside the machine and never removed his hand from the switch until he saw I would continue breathing on my own. I missed the first couple of breaths after he turned the machine off but then felt God breathe into my lungs His breath of life.

The doctor and nurses watched me for almost ten minutes, until they thought I would continue breathing on my own.

For the next several hours the surgeon required that one of the nurses be posted by that machine watching me breathe, so it could be turned on in a matter of seconds if need be. He came in to check on me three more times that day, and each time he yanked on the drainage tubes he had inserted around my liver. These tubes were coming out of a hole in my abdomen the surgeon had created. The reason he yanked on them was so the skin would not adhere to the tubes. This yanking three or four times a day was necessary, but very painful.

You Can't Kill a Dead Man

Early Wednesday morning the surgeon came in wearing a shirt and tie and lab coat as he had done on Tuesday. He first asked the nurse by my bed how I had done overnight with my breathing.

"Great," she responded. "His breathing has gotten stronger throughout the night, and I think he's breathing deeper than he has since the surgery."

With that report the doctor ordered that the breathing tube apparatus and stomach tube be removed from my nose and mouth. After a quick, painful yank on the drainage tubes, he was off to other responsibilities.

Having the tube removed from my nose and stomach was the worst part of that process. However, it also eliminated the cause of my sore throat, which was a huge relief. Being able to drink, eat, and talk was the biggest blessing from that freedom-giving procedure.

Sometime after breakfast I looked up and saw the surgeon come into the ward again. This time he was wearing his suit jacket instead of his lab coat. I started to prepare mentally for the pain of him yanking on the drainage tubes, but he shocked me when he sat down on the edge of my bed.

"You're doing really good, you know," he said to me. "You're going to make it!"

I smiled slightly and nodded, grateful for the confirmation of what I already knew.

"When I got to you," he hesitantly went on, "it was too late. From where your vein was torn open you should have bled to death in thirty to forty-five minutes at the most, but you're still alive."

I listened intently as he struggled to reconcile his medical knowledge with the fact that I was alive.

"When I got to you," his face showed anguish, "no blood was flowing through your veins. You had completely bled out into your body cavity. I had to put back every ounce of blood into your body, a total transfusion. Yet you're still alive. I don't understand it! I don't understand why you are alive!"

"I know why," I prepared to tell him about hearing God promise me that it would be all right.

"Yeah, yeah, I know," he interrupted my thought process. "It's because God kept you alive. I know that! There could be no other explanation."

Over his shoulder I saw one of the nurses who was walking back to her nurse's station stop when the doctor said that. She turned her head slightly toward us to listen as she slowly kept moving to her station.

"I'll be back to check on you later," the doctor patted me on the leg then left the ward.

As soon as he was gone, that nurse hurried over to my bed. "Did he say what I thought he said?"

"I don't know," I responded. "What did you think he said?"

"Did he say," she hurried to respond, "that the only reason you are alive is God?"

"Yeah, he did," I answered.

"You've got to be kidding me!" She squealed. "Do you know who he is?"

"Not really," I answered.

"He's a well-known published agnostic!" she reported.

"Not anymore," I smiled.

"No," she said then smiled. "Not anymore!" With that she returned to her station.

About an hour later a black man dressed in a shirt, tie, and sports jacket came into the ward and came straight to my bed. He introduced himself as the doctor in charge of the ER the night that I was brought in to the hospital.

"You probably don't recognize me," he went on, "since you were pretty out of it that night."

I truly didn't remember him.

"When we got to you," he said as he also sat on the edge of my bed, "it was completely too late for us to save you. But I've seen God do miracles like that before."

I smiled at the second medical confirmation that my survival was indeed a miracle from God.

"But what I hadn't seen before," he continued, "were the two things God did for you while you were waiting for surgery."

"What were they?" I asked.

"Well," he said, "the first thing is that you never lost consciousness even while waiting more than three hours for surgery. And the second thing is you never went into shock even after losing all your blood. That's unheard of!"

"I believe I know why these miracles happened to me," I said to that doctor.

"Why is that?" he responded.

"Well," I tried to explain, "when I was in Vietnam I 'killed myself' by giving my life to Jesus Christ. And Galatians 2:20 says I am dead or 'crucified with Christ. Nevertheless, I live' or it appears that I am alive even though I am dead. 'Yet not I, but Christ, liveth in me.' It's not me living; it's Jesus living His life in me. You see, when I no longer had my blood flowing through my veins, I had His blood flowing through me. Besides, "I paused and looked right at him, "all this proves you can't kill a dead man!"

CHAPTER ONE

"THE TWO MOST POWERFUL EXPRESSIONS OF WORSHIP"

MUSIC: A POWERFUL EXPRESSION OF WORSHIP

When we hear the word *worship* we usually think of music. Most people think that *worship* and *music* are interchangeable. Have you ever wondered why?

In *Portrait of a Worshiper* I listed thirty-four[3] Biblical expressions of worship that our body can do to express our love to Almighty God. Only two of those thirty-four expressions are musical—playing musical instruments and singing. Why, then, is music the most-used expression of worship in our Christian gatherings? Why isn't shouting or dancing or laying prostrate the most popular expressions of Christian worship when we get together?

Let me begin to answer these questions by stating two facts. First, music (including singing) is the most powerful expression of worship that God has given to us for our gatherings.

Second, the Bible commands us to sing and make melody or music.

Here are just a few of the scriptures that command us to sing and play musical instruments as an expression of praise to our God.

> *Serve the Lord with gladness: come before His presence with singing. Psalm 100:2 (KJV)*

---

[3] Portrait of a Worshiper pages 122-126

Sing praises to God, sing praises: sing praises unto our King, sing praises. For God is the King of all the earth: sing ye praises with understanding. Psalm 47:6-7 (KJV)

Praise Him with the sound of the trumpet: praise Him with the psaltery and harp. Praise Him with the timbrel and dance: praise Him with stringed instruments and organs. Praise Him upon the loud cymbals: praise Him upon the high-sounding cymbals. Let everything that hath breath praise the Lord. Praise ye the Lord. Psalm 150:3-6 (KJV)

Speaking to yourselves in psalms and hymns and spiritual songs, singing and making melody in your heart to the Lord; Ephesians 5:19 (KJV)

Let the word of Christ dwell in you richly in all wisdom; teaching and admonishing one another in psalms and hymns and spiritual songs, singing with grace in your hearts to the Lord. Colossians 3:16 (KJV)

We sing and make music as an expression of our love and worship of God because God commanded it, and because He created it to be the most powerful expression of worship for us in the gathering of believers.

AN OVERVIEW OF CHURCH HISTORY

It was not called the Dark Ages for nothing. During that dark period in church history, every truth God had established in His early church was lost and perverted, including worship.

The crowning glory of Catholic music in the Dark Ages came into form about 600 A.D. during the reign of Pope Gregory. To this day this type of music is referred to as the Gregorian Chant. It is called a chant because the melody of these songs usually stayed on one note and only deviated from that note toward the end of each lyrical or musical phrase.

Nothing much changed in worship music until the Reformation, the period in church history marked by Martin Luther and John Calvin. God used these two men to change Christianity forever.

Martin Luther wrote his ninety-nine-point theses to restore several fundamental Christian truths, especially the truth that is found in these scriptures.

> *For by grace are ye saved through faith; and that not of yourselves: it is the gift of God: Not of works, lest any man should boast. Ephesians 2:8-9 (KJV)*

> *For therein is the righteousness of God revealed from faith to faith: as it is written, The just shall live by faith. Romans 1:17 (KJV)*

> *But that no man is justified by the law in the sight of God, it is evident: for, The just shall live by faith. Galatians 3:11 (KJV)*

> *Now the just shall live by faith: but if any man draw back, My soul shall have no pleasure in him. Hebrews 10:38 (KJV)*

Along with this restored truth of salvation coming to us through faith (not works), the Reformation is also known as when God restored worship music back to the people. The Gregorian chant style was characterized by priests chanting parts of the Catholic mass to the people. Luther and Calvin received revelations from God regarding worship being sung by the people of God. For the first time in hundreds of years, singing and the making of music was released back to the people through these men of God.

A controversy, however, arose between Luther and Calvin due to differences about worship style. John Calvin believed that the only texts through which we should worship God should come from scripture—specifically, the Book of Psalms. Martin Luther, on the other hand, believed that more genuine worship occurred when texts of human composition were used.

I believe both of these men were right. Today most of us sing both types of worship songs to God. It is a shame when truth that God intends to bring us into unity divides us.

Since God used Martin Luther to begin His restoration of truths back to His church, God has methodically restored truths to His people throughout history. Here's an overview of these restored truths throughout history.

An Overview of Restored Truths

Who God Used	What God Restored
Martin Luther	Salvation by faith *Ephesians 2:8*
John Calvin	God's sovereignty *Romans 8:28-31*
Anabaptists	Baptism by emersion *Matthew 3:15-17*
John and Charles Wesley	Holiness through discipline and methodology *1 Peter 1:13-16*
William Carey	Foreign missions *Acts 1:8*
Billy Sunday, Charles Finney, Dr. Billy Graham	Evangelism of the masses *Acts 2:40-41*
William Seymour Azusa Street Revival	Signs and wonders, healings, and the baptism of the Holy Spirit *Mark 16:17-20*
North Battleford, Saskatchewan, Canada The Latter Rain Movement	The gifts of the Holy Spirit and singing with the Spirit *Joel 2:23*
The Charismatic Movement	The baptism of the Holy Spirit for all denominations *Acts 2:17-19*
Rodney Howard Brown, The Toronto Blessing, The Brownsville Revival	The Joy of the Lord from the intoxicating presence of God *Acts 2:12-16*

Rob Skiba, Johnathan Cahn, The Internet	Truth about creation, cosmology, heaven, signs in the heavens, and decoded Biblical messages *Genesis 1*

Table I

Just like God restored significant truth about singing praise and worship to Martin Luther, He also revealed more revelation about worship each time he restored other Biblical truths. Martin Luther gave us the ability to write and sing hymns. John Calvin gave us the singing of psalms and other scriptures. John and Charles Wesley increased the singing of songs and hymns. After Charles Wesley was converted, it was reported that he wrote the words and many of the melodies to more than 6,500 multiple-verse hymns.

Every great revivalist had their song leaders. Charles Wesley was to John Wesley what Cliff Barrows was to Billy Graham. They were not called worship leaders until the late 1970s.

It was in North Battleford, Saskatchewan, Canada at a church camp in 1948 when Christians first experienced what we call spontaneous worship for the first time. Some people call this "singing in the Spirit." This style of worship is where the singers and instrumentalists allow the Holy Spirit to spontaneously give them the melody, words, and chords has become the norm for the International House of Prayer in Grandview, Missouri, where they alternate this type of prophetic worship with prayer twenty-four hours a day, seven days a week. They call it the "harp and bowl" style of worship based on this scripture in Revelation.

> *Now when He had taken the scroll, the four living creatures and the twenty-four elders fell down before the Lamb, each having a **harp**, **and** golden **bowls** full of incense, which are the prayers of the saints. And they sang a new song, saying: "You are worthy to take the scroll, And to open its seals; For You were slain, And have redeemed us to God by Your blood Out of every tribe and tongue and people and nation, And have made us kings and priests to our God;*

And we shall reign on the earth." Revelation 5:8-10 (NKJV)
emphasis added

On and on we could go rehearsing the restoration of worship music alongside the revelation of Godly truths throughout church history. With that being understood, it begs the question again as to why God equates music with unified worship? This correlation between music and worship is also seen in the Old Testament as well.

Again, aren't the playing of musical instruments and singing only two of the thirty-four different Biblical expressions of worship? We need to find out what makes music so special to make it the consistent group expression of worship throughout history and the Bible.

THE EXPRESSOR OF OUR WORSHIP

God created us for the express purpose of worshiping Him.[4] The way He created us has everything to do with us accomplishing that purpose. He made us in three parts: spirit, soul, and body.[5] Therefore, each part is important in carrying out our purpose.

In *Portrait of a Worshiper* I outlined the function of our three parts when we worship Jesus. The spirit of man joined to God's Spirit becomes the initiator of our worship. Our body is the expressor of our worship. And, since our body is controlled in every way by our mind (part of our soul), the soul must be in tune with the Spirit so our body is following the leading of the Spirit. We call our soul the "conductor" of our worship, in the sense of electricity, because the soul is the place where all the short circuits can occur.

Since our spirit requires our body to express itself, it is not Biblical for us to say, "I worship God in my spirit only," as an excuse not to express worship with our body. By using the list of Biblical worship expressions that we created in *Portrait of a Worshiper*, we can see very quickly that God intended for us to use our bodies to express what is in our heart or spirit. For instance, our spirit cannot kneel as an expression of worship—it has no knees without our body. Our spirit cannot bow—it has no waist except

---

[4] Isaiah 43:21
[5] 1 Thessalonians 5:23

on our body. Our spirit cannot dance—it has no feet without our body. Our spirit cannot clap—it has no hands. Our Spirit cannot shout—it has no mouth. Our spirit requires the use of our body to fulfill the purpose for which we were created. What is in our heart must be expressed with our body.

THE EXCEPTIONS TO THIS RULE

When I studied music in university, I took two years of music theory and learned the correct rules for writing music. One of the strictest rules was never to use parallel fifths or octaves. For two years these rules were drilled into our heads. Then came the third year of music theory when we learned how to break every rule we had spent the last two years learning. We asked our professor why we spent the last two years learning all the music theory rules if we were just going to break them. She answered, "You have to know the rules before you can learn how and when to apply the exceptions to them."

Now that we have reviewed the rule that every worship expression in the Bible is done by our body, I would like to share with you the two exceptions to this rule.

> *What is the conclusion then? I will pray with the spirit, and I will also pray with the understanding. I will sing with the spirit, and I will also sing with the understanding. 1 Corinthians 14:15 (NKJV)*

In chapters 12, 13, and 14 of First Corinthians Paul is addressing spiritual gifts. Chapter 12 outlines what the spiritual gifts are. Chapter 13 explains that the spiritual gifts must be operated from a heart of love, humility, and respect for others. Chapter 14 explains how these spiritual gifts should work in the church.

Throughout many of his books in the New Testament Paul uses a literary technique called a "summit conclusion" in which he presents a concluding statement before reaching the end of his topic. These statements allow readers to see and understand both where he has been and where he is going.

In the middle of all of Paul's practical instruction about the gifts of the

Holy Spirit in chapter 14, Paul gives us this extremely important summit conclusion, which I have paraphrased below.

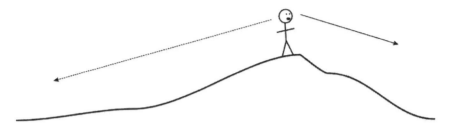

> *"I'm trying to teach you how to operate the gifts of the Holy Spirit, so let me summarize this whole process for you. Operating the gifts of the Spirit works the same way we pray and sing. We can pray and sing with just our natural understanding, or we can pray and sing with just our spirit only. But what I want you to do is to pray and sing with both your spirit and your natural understanding at the same time. Now, if you can understand this, that is the way all spiritual gifts operate."* 1 Corinthians 14:15 (paraphrased by Shamblin Stone)

THE TWO MOST POWERFUL EXPRESSIONS OF WORSHIP

In trying to explain the way the gifts of the Holy Spirit operate, Paul has let us in on an important secret about worship. Every Biblical expression of worship requires that our bodies be the expressors, yet there are two expressions of worship that do not require our bodies to express them: prayer and singing. These two are the only expressions of worship which can be done by our spirit, without the aid of our body. This fact separates these two worship expressions from all the others and qualifies them to be called the most powerful worship expressions found in the Bible. Here is a chart to help you visualize this Biblical concept.

1 Corinthians 14:15 at a Glance

PRAY	**WITH**	SPIRIT
SING		UNDERSTANDING

Table II

UNDERSTANDING OUR UNDERSTANDING

First introduced in *Portrait of a Worshiper*, here is a review of this fundamental truth:

1. Mankind was designed and created in three parts: spirit, soul, and body.[6]

2. Jesus redeemed or purchased all three parts of our being back to Himself with His own blood.[7]

3. Our spirit is the only part of our being that has been saved.[8] Our soul is undergoing the process of salvation in this earthly lifetime[9], and our body is waiting for the day of "Adoption"[10] when it will be changed to be like Christ's glorified body.[11]

4. Because of this, the Bible considers our spirit as the "spiritual man" and the un-regenerated soul and body as the "natural man."[12]

5. Natural "understanding" involves a human being's body and soul. It is impossible for the natural man to understand the things of the spirit.

> *But the natural man receiveth not the things of the Spirit of God: for they are foolishness unto him: neither can he know them, because they are spiritually discerned. 1 Corinthians 2:14 (KJV)*

---

[6] 1 Thessalonians 5:23
[7] 1 Corinthians 6:19-20
[8] 1 Corinthians 6:17
[9] Philippians 2:12
[10] Romans 8:21-23
[11] Philippians 3:21
[12] Romans 7:18

6. Natural understanding is gained by receiving data through the five senses and processing that data in the three parts of our soul.

Let me expand this last point in a little more detail. We gain understanding by following these steps.

1. Step One: Gather data from the five senses (our body)
   a. What do I see?
   b. What do I hear?
   c. What do I smell?
   d. What do I taste?
   e. What am I touching?
2. Step Two: Process the data with our soul and reach these conclusions
   a. What do I think about this? (mind)
   b. How do I feel about this? (emotions)
   c. What will I do about this? (will)

A wise person will add a third step to the gaining of understanding.

3. Step Three: Share my conclusions with a friend for balance and input then adjust my conclusions accordingly
   a. What do they think about my conclusions in this matter?
   b. How do they feel about my conclusions in this matter?
   c. What would they do in this situation?

Also, a spiritual person will add a fourth step to the gaining of understanding.

4. Step Four: Seek spiritual input and adjust my conclusions accordingly
   a. What does the Word of God have to say about this matter?
   b. What is the leading of the Holy Spirit in this matter?

Finally, a mature person will add a fifth step to the gaining of understanding.

5. Step Five: Observe the results of my conclusions for future conclusions
   a. Was what I thought correct?
   b. Was what I felt correct?
   c. Was what I did correct?

The first two steps outlined above for gaining understanding involve both our bodies and our souls, the un-regenerated parts of our being. Therefore, we conclude that Paul is saying in 1 Corinthians 14:15 that we can pray and sing with the natural part of us—the body and soul—and we can pray and sing with the spiritual part of us, our spirit.

Praying and Singing on Both Levels

To pray with the understanding can happen this way. We may see somebody in need or hear of somebody in need and imagine what it would be like with that need. By thinking about that person's situation, we may be touched emotionally by that need and finally decide to ask God to meet that person's need. That would be considered as praying with our understanding, motivated by our understanding.

I went to university to learn to sing with understanding. I majored in vocal pedagogy, which is the study of the proper way to sing. I learned all about rhythm, harmony, and melody so I could read music that is written and sing it or play it. Now I understand how to sing properly, and I can also teach others what I know. Both praying and singing with the understanding are done with our body and soul, and these acts are not initiated in our spirit.

Before I talk about what it means to pray and sing with the spirit, let me remind you that a Christian's spirit has been joined to the Holy Spirit, and the two spirits have become one spirit.

> But he that is joined unto the Lord is one spirit. 1 Corinthians 6:17 (KJV)

Praying with our spirit is described for us in this scripture.

> *Likewise the Spirit also helpeth our infirmities: for we know not what we should pray for as we ought: but the Spirit itself maketh intercession for us with groanings which cannot be uttered. Romans 8:26 (KJV)*

I have often heard this scripture used as validation for speaking in tongues. With a simple word study, we find that using this scripture in that way is incorrect. The English phrase *"groanings which cannot be uttered"* is the Greek word transliterated as "alaletos." It is Strong's Greek word 215 and is defined as "inexpressible, or unable to be expressed, unspeakable—unutterable, which cannot be uttered." The NAS Exhaustive Concordance defines it as "too deep for words." The Thayer's Greek Lexicon defines it as "not to be uttered, not to be expressed in words: mute sighs."[13]

What this scripture is describing is the Spirit praying without using the body to make any sound at all, including the forming of audible words. Speaking in tongues is audible and is heard by others in the vicinity of those who are speaking in tongues.

> *Now when this was noised abroad, the multitude came together, and were confounded, because that every man heard them speak in his own language. And they were all amazed and marveled, saying one to another, Behold, are not all these which speak Galilaeans? And how hear we every man in our own tongue, wherein we were born? Acts 2:6-8 (KJV)*

Therefore, Romans 8:26 is not describing tongues, but it is describing the spirit praying without the aid of the body.

Singing with our spirit is described in this scripture as "making melody in our heart."

> *And be not drunk with wine, wherein is excess; but be filled with the Spirit; Speaking to yourselves in psalms and hymns and spiritual songs, singing and making melody in your heart to the Lord; Ephesians 5:18-19 (KJV)*

---

[13] Bible Hub Strong's Greek: 215 retrieved 1-16-2020

Just as it is possible for the human heart or spirit to pray to God without making an audible sound in the natural realm, so it is possible for our spirit to sing without making an audible sound. Such a song can only be detected by another spirit.

Although it is possible to pray to God with only our spirit and with only our understanding, when Paul used the word "also" in 1 Corinthians 14:15 it indicates that he wants us to pray with our understanding and our spirit at the same time whenever possible. Likewise, he used the word "also" in his instructions for us to sing with our spirit as well as our understanding, meaning he wants us to do them at the same time as much as possible.

Again, I remind you that praying and singing are the only two expressions of worship that can be done with only our spirit. All other expressions of worship require our bodies to express them.

There is no deeper communication known to mankind than to commune spirit to Spirit with God! This is why prayer is the most powerful expression of individual worship given to mankind.

In a group setting of worship, however, God has ordained that we "come before His presence with singing."[14] Music was created by God to be a unifying factor for the Body of Christ both levels—spirit and natural understanding. Just like prayer is communion with God on a spirit-to-Spirit level, music can both originate in and transcend to the human spirit as well as to God's Spirit. God designed music to do this so we could experience the greatest unity possible within a setting of worshiping together.

Learning to Pray With Our Spirit

You may just now be awakening to the fact that your spirit can pray without the aid of your body. If so, then you are probably wondering how you are going to learn to pray with your spirit. Fortunately, God has given us a way for us to learn this very thing.

---

[14] Psalm 100:2

> *For if I pray in an unknown tongue, my spirit prayeth,*
> *but my understanding is unfruitful. 1 Corinthians 14:14*
> *(KJV)*

The reason for speaking in tongues has always been to teach us to pray with our spirit, not with our understanding. Once we learn to pray with our spirit by praying in tongues, we will be able to pray with our spirit without the aid of our body.

In the 1980s I was fortunate enough to speak to most of the chapters of the Full Gospel Businessmen's Fellowship International (FGBMFI) throughout western Canada and at many of the organization's conventions. After presenting my testimony at a meeting for the Prince George (British Columbia) chapter, I invited anyone who desired prayer for any reason to come stand at the front of the banquet hall where we were assembled. The line for prayer stretched all the way across the front. I started at my far left, praying for each person individually. Some I would ask for them to tell me what they wanted prayer for. Others, I would simply let the Holy Spirit tell me what to pray for (praying prophetically).

There was an older woman in a wheelchair in the prayer line, with a younger woman standing behind her. When I came to her in the line, I began to speak in an unknown language, unlike any other prayer language I had ever spoken in.

After praying for a few minutes in that language, I moved to the next person in the line, again speaking in English and another unknown language. I was privileged to pray for thirty to forty people that night, but the only one that I didn't pray for in English was the woman in the wheelchair. I didn't think much about that until a few months went by.

About eight months later I was about to leave the hospital after vising someone from my church there when a woman waiting to get on the elevator stopped me.

"You're Shamblin Stone," she said.

"That's right," I responded, stopping to talk to her. "How do you know me?"

"Do you remember about eight months ago," she began, "when you spoke at the Full Gospel Businessmen's meeting?"

When I responded in the affirmative, she continued. "Do you remember praying for an elderly woman in a wheelchair at that meeting?"

"Yes, I do," I responded.

"That woman is my mother, and I was standing behind her in the prayer line," she continued. "How many languages do you speak?"

"I only know English," I responded.

"My mother is from the Ukraine, and she can't speak a word of English. When you came to her in the prayer line, you prayed for her in perfect Ukrainian. My mother understood every word."

That piqued my curiosity. "Well, what did I pray?"

"You blessed her with long life, and you asked Jesus to reveal to her how much He loves her."

Because I knew how to pray with my spirit, the Lord was able to pray for that woman through me in the language she understood without me even knowing it was happening.

Please do not be deceived into thinking that speaking in tongues is only for a few people. In the book of Acts, everyone who asked for it received it. If speaking in tongues is the way God has given us to learn how to pray with our spirit, why would he give that gift to only a select few? The answer is, He wouldn't. He wants every one of us to speak in tongues.

> ***I wish you all spoke with tongues***, *but even more that you prophesied; for he who prophesies is greater than he who speaks with tongues, unless indeed he interprets, that the church may receive edification. 1 Corinthians 14:5 (NKJV) emphasis added*

Being able to pray with our spirit is a very encouraging experience. The King James Version of the Bible calls that "edifying."

> *He that speaketh in an unknown tongue edifieth himself; but he that prophesieth edifieth the church. 1 Corinthians 14:4 (KJV)*

God would not want some to be able to edify themselves and others unable to, which is why He gives the gift of tongues to every person who asks for it.

SINGING WITH THE SPIRIT

How do we recognize when someone is singing with their spirit and understanding simultaneously? Perhaps you've encountered those who have had several years of voice training and have polished their singing skills with their understanding. As they sing, we, with our understanding, can appreciate the skill level they have obtained vocally from the many years of hard work. Yet, with many of these people their music does not move us on a deeper spiritual level.

Then a dear saint gets up to sing for church one day. She has no vocal training. She breathes in all the wrong places. Her vowel sounds are inconsistent. She goes flat on every other note. Yet, when she sings, we're touched deep within. The world calls this "singing from the heart." The Bible calls it "singing with the spirit." Our spirit receives her spirit's song. That is why her song touches us so deeply.

Humanity's ability to pray and sing with our spirit makes prayer and music the two most unique and most powerful expressions of worship which God has given to us.

PRAYING "IN THE SPIRIT"

There is a difference between praying with the spirit and praying "in" the spirit. Both are Biblical phrases which mean two different things. These phrases are not interchangeable.

There are only two places in the New Testament where the phrase "praying in the Spirit" occurs.

> *But you, beloved, building yourselves up on your most holy faith, praying **in** the Holy Spirit. Jude :20 (NKJV) emphasis added*

> *praying always with all prayer and supplication **in** the Spirit, being watchful to this end with all perseverance*

and supplication for all the saints Ephesians 6:18 (NKJV)
emphasis added

When we study the original Greek texts for these scriptures, we can see that neither of these scriptures indicate speaking in tongues.

According to HELPS Word-studies™ the word "in" in these scriptures is Strong's Greek word 1722 and means "in the realm (sphere) of, as in the condition (state) in which something operates from."[15] These scriptures indicate the petitioning of God from a spiritual position of understanding spiritual truths concerning our authority Christ has given to us.

"In the Spirit" is a position while "with the Spirit" is an action. Perhaps it would be important for us to review the difference between the Spirit in us and us in Him.

Before we can understand the position of us "in the Spirit," we need to understand the position of the Spirit IN-side us. This position of the Spirit of Christ in us was promised to the worshipers of God by Jesus Himself. Until Jesus came, this was not available to mankind.

> *And I will pray the Father, and He shall give you another*
> *Comforter, that He may abide with you forever; Even the*
> *Spirit of truth; whom the world cannot receive, because it*
> *seeth Him not, neither knoweth Him: but ye know Him; for*
> *He dwelleth **with** you, and shall be **in** you. John 14:16-17*
> *(KJV) emphasis added*

The Spirit of God in us was a mystery until Jesus came to reveal God to us.

> *To them God willed to make known what are the riches*
> *of the glory of this mystery among the Gentiles: which is*
> *Christ **in** you, the hope of glory. Colossians 1:27 (NKJV)*
> *emphasis added*

As we said, the Spirit in us was not given to the Old Testament saints.

---

[15] Bible Hub Strong's Greek: 1722 retrieved 1-17-2020

That is a privileged promise reserved for those who come to God through Jesus.

> *And all these, having obtained a good testimony through faith, did not receive **the promise**, God having provided something better for us, that they should not be made perfect apart from us. Hebrews 11:39-40 (NKJV) emphasis added*

When we receive Jesus Christ as our Lord, He gives us the Holy Spirit, which He promised to put within us.

> *In Him you also trusted, after you heard the word of truth, the gospel of your salvation; in whom also, having believed, you were sealed with the Holy **Spirit of promise**, who is the guarantee of our inheritance until the redemption of the purchased possession, to the praise of His glory. Ephesians 1:13-14 (NKJV) emphasis added*

When we speak of the Spirit within us, we mean inside our body.

> *Or do you not know that your body is the temple of the Holy Spirit who is **in you**, whom you have from God, and you are not your own? For you were bought at a price; therefore, glorify God in your body and in your spirit, which are God's. 1 Corinthians 6:19-20 (NKJV) emphasis added*

The Spirit of God "in us" is the first step toward us moving into the position of being "in the Spirit." The Spirit "in us" is the promise that we will be "in the Spirit" at some time in the future.

Let's review what the positional statement "in the Spirit" means and how we get there.

> *But the anointing which you have received from Him abides **in you**, and you do not need that anyone teach you; but as the same anointing teaches you concerning all things, and is true, and is not a lie, and just as it has taught you, you will abide **in Him**. 1 John 2:27 (NKJV) emphasis added*

The anointing is the Holy Spirit which the Father has given to us. It is the anointing who teaches us all spiritual things. Here is what Jesus himself said about this subject:

> *But the Helper, the Holy Spirit, whom the Father will send in My name, He will teach you all things, and bring to your remembrance all things that I said to you. John 14:26 (NKJV)*

Look at how well these two scriptures fit on top of each other. That is because they were written by the same human author, and the same Holy Spirit.

The Spirit is Our Teacher

1 John 2:27	John 14:26
But the Anointing . . . abides in you	*But the Helper, the Holy Spirit,*
which you have received from Him	*whom the Father will send in My name*
the same anointing teaches you concerning all things	*He will teach you all things*

Table III

1 John 2:27 is the clearest Scripture we have which teaches the difference between the Spirit in us and us in the Spirit. The Spirit in us happens when we make Jesus Lord of our lives. Us in the Spirit happens when we allow the Spirit of God to teach us. To the degree we allow the Spirit to teach us is the degree that we are "in" Him."

Notice the progression which occurs in this verse, and what it takes for this progression to take place.

> *But the anointing which you have received from Him abides **in you** . . . as it has taught you, you will abide **in Him**. 1 John 2:27 (NKJV) emphasis added*

We move from Christ being in us to us being in Christ when we let the Holy Spirit teach us according to the Word of Truth. And, to the degree that He has taught us, old things have passed away, and in the areas where the holy spirit has taught us, those things become new.

> *Therefore, **if** anyone is **in Christ**, he is a new creation;*
> *old things have passed away; behold, all things have become*
> *new. 2 Corinthians 5:17 (NKJV) emphasis added*

In Vietnam when I first gave my life to Jesus, someone quoted this scripture to me and told me I was now a new creation. They told me all the old sin in my life was gone and that everything was new. The problem was, the very next day I experienced some of the same old fleshly lusts and desires I had always had. I became very confused. No one explained to me that old things passing away and all things becoming new is a process, not an automatic event, and this promise is conditional.

The biggest word in the English language has only two letters. It is the word *if*. In 2 Corinthians 5:17, the prerequisite for old things passing away and all things becoming new is that we must be in Christ. That means if we are not in Christ, the old things have not passed away and things have not become new.

To be "in Christ" means we have allowed the Holy Spirit to teach us spiritual truths. In those things which the Holy Spirit has taught us, we are "in Christ." In those things only have the old ways passed away, and we have become new creatures. To the level that the Holy Spirit has taught us in those areas of our lives we have become "in Christ."

Some of us are "in the Spirit" more than others because we have allowed Him to be our teacher more than others have. But we all have the same potential of being "in the Spirit." It is up to us as to how much we allow the Lord to teach us.

So then, praying in the Spirit is praying from a position of revelation knowledge which we have been taught by the Holy Spirit. It is praying from a position of faith birthed in us by revelation from the Holy Spirit teaching us the Word of Truth.

> *So then faith comes by hearing, and hearing by the word*
> *of God. Romans 10:17 (NKJV)*

Praying in the Spirit is praying from a position of authority and power, which is discovered through the revelation knowledge brought by the Spirit of Christ. Singing "in" the Spirit would be the same thing, if that were a Biblical phrase, which it is not.

Prayer Is to Individual Worship . . .

Prayer is for communicating with God one-on-one, spirit to Spirit, heart to Heart. While it is true that prayer can be done in a group setting, it must be adapted from an individual communication media to a group-dynamic communication tool to be effective in the group setting.

There are only two Biblical ways to use prayer in the group setting. First, prayer can be done by many people all at the same time. This could be in tongues or in a known language. This type of group prayer is simply individuals praying to God on their own at the same time as everyone else within a group setting. This type of group prayer makes it difficult to understand what anyone is praying. Such a group prayer can portray chaos to the unbelievers who may be in attendance.

> *If therefore the whole church be come together into one place, and all speak with tongues, and there come in those that are unlearned, or unbelievers, will they not say that ye are mad? 1 Corinthians 14:23 (KJV)*

The other Biblical way prayer can be used in the group setting is to have one person pray audibly, with their understanding, and everyone else in the room simply agrees with that prayer. This is the most-often used form of prayer in group settings because it is the most orderly. However, this prayer is still done by an individual.

> *Again I say to you that if two of you agree on earth concerning anything that they ask, it will be done for them by My Father in heaven. Matthew 18:19 (NKJV)*

Prayer was designed by God as spirit-to-Spirit communication between one person and God. That is prayer's purpose. This is why God created prayer to be done with our spirit without the aid of our bodies so that our spirits can commune with God's Spirit on a deep, spiritual level.

Prayer is always to be a two-way conversation—spirit to Spirit, which makes it the most powerful expression of worship between one person and the Lord. We should strive to get to the place where our prayers are always communicated simultaneously with our spirit and our understanding at the same time.

. . . WHAT MUSIC IS TO WORSHIPING TOGETHER

God designed music (or singing) for the group setting. Here's why I say that. In Paul's writings he makes it clear that unity in our gatherings is absolutely essential.

> *Fulfill My joy by being **like-minded**, having the **same love**, being of **one accord**, of **one mind**. Philippians 2:2 (NKJV) emphasis added*

> *Now I plead with you, brethren, by the name of our Lord Jesus Christ, that you all **speak the same thing**, and that there be **no divisions** among you, but that you be **perfectly joined together** in the **same mind** and in the **same judgment**. 1 Corinthians 1:10 (NKJV) emphasis added*

Before I talk about these verses, let me say this: There are two basic ways to exegete all Scripture. One way is to take the Scriptures literally or figuratively. Those who interpret Scriptures figuratively will say that Jonah did not actually spend three days in the belly of the great fish. I, however, believe that was a literal event—and that every event in the Bible literally happened. Daniel spent the night in the Lion's den. The Hebrew children spent time in an actual furnace and survived. Jesus actually died on a wooden cross and rose from the dead. If you take the Bible figuratively, you can pick and choose what you want to believe. To me that is a dangerous position, so I choose to believe every part of the Bible as literal.

We are encouraged in the Scriptures to both "be of one mind," and to "speak the same thing." If we take the Scriptures literally, the only way we can obey these commandments is with music. When we sing together, we are not only "speaking" the same things, but we are speaking them at the exact same time together. The lyrics of a song provide us with the way to speak the same thing, and the rhythmic structure of a song provides us with the way to speak the same thing at the same time.

Without rhythm found in music, it is impossible for a group of people to say the exact same thing at the exact same time. Even when people recite the Lord's Prayer together in a group setting, a scripted prayer, we never end up saying the words exactly at the same time. Somebody always speeds up or slows down, and we never do it the same way twice. At the end of the prayer you will hear numerous "Amens" no matter how hard the group tries to end it together.

But if you sing it, you will end it together almost every time, even without rehearsal. That's the nature of music.

There's another aspect to music which helps us "be of the same mind" and even to feel or express the same emotions at the same time. The melody of the song we are singing provides this. In every language of the world, the expression of emotions when we talk is reflected through the different pitches we speak with. Changing the pitches changes the emotions being expressed and the entire meaning of the words.

Below I have written the same words several times. I want you to read these words out loud, trying to vary the pitches of each word according to what I have indicated above the word. For this exercise, the pitches you use do not need to be exact, as though you are singing a melody. Simply move the pitches on each word in the direction indicated to the best of your ability. After you have said each phrase, before reading further, try to guess what that phrase is saying using that set of pitches. Then read on to see how close your interpretation is to mine.

This exercise is meant to show how we can say the same words in several different ways with totally different meanings. By changing the pitches on the different words, we can say things that the words themselves do not say.

Multiple Meaning Exercise

INSTRUCTIONS: Say these phrases below out loud, changing the pitch of your voice to generally match the pitches indicated above the words.

Phrase #1

			▓		
▓		▓			
	▓			▓	▓
I	think	I	like	your	dress.

Table IV

I like your dress, but I do not love it.

Phrase #2

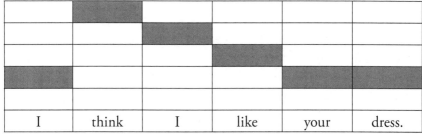

	▓				
		▓			
			▓		
▓				▓	▓
I	think	I	like	your	dress.

Table V

I might like your dress but I am not sure.

Phrase #3

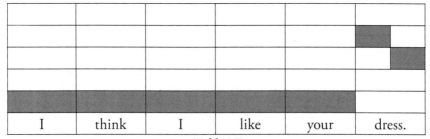

					▓
					▓
▓	▓	▓	▓	▓	
I	think	I	like	your	dress.

Table VI

Your dress is all right, but your shoes are ridiculous.

Phrase #4

I	think	I	like	your	dress.

Table VII

I am trying to convince myself that I like your dress.

Phrase #5

I	think	I	like	your	dress.

Table VIII

I am probably the only one who likes your dress.

This is how song melodies affect the meaning of the lyrics. When we sing together, we speak the very same thing, at the same time, expressing the same emotions or actual meaning of the words we are singing, and we can do it from our heart or spirit. No other expression given to us by God can provide this depth of instant unity.

This is why we worship God through singing and music whenever we get together as a church—because music is the most powerful expression of unified worship God has given to us, just like prayer is the most powerful expression of worship we have been given as individuals. Music is to worshiping together what prayer is to individual worship.

THE IMPORTANCE OF UNITY

There are two Scriptures I would like to share with you which define for us how important unity is when we worship together.

> *Behold, how good and how pleasant it is for brethren to dwell **together in unity**! It is like the precious ointment upon the head, that ran down upon the beard, even Aaron's beard: that went down to the skirts of his garments; As the dew of Hermon, and as the dew that descended upon the mountains of Zion: for **there the Lord commanded the blessing**, even life for evermore. Psalm 133:1-3 (KJV) emphasis added*

There is nothing more important to human existence than the blessing of Almighty God. It really doesn't matter what life throws at us as long as we live under the blessing of the Almighty. This scripture clearly teaches us that the way to have the blessing of God is to dwell in unity with our brethren.

The second scripture comes at this subject from a negative position; however, we can still learn a positive lesson from it. It happened in the story of the Tower of Babel. Do you recall how everyone decided to build a tower to reach to the heavens? We're picking up the story halfway through it in the New Living Translation of the Bible.

> *But the Lord came down to look at the city and the tower the people were building. "Look!" He said. "**The people are united**, and they all speak the same language. After this, **nothing they set out to do will be impossible for them!** Come, let's go down and confuse the people with different languages. Then they won't be able to understand each other."*
>
> *In that way, the Lord scattered them all over the world, and they stopped building the city. That is why the city was called Babel, because that is where the Lord confused the people with different languages. In this way he scattered them all over the world. Genesis 11:5-9 (NLT) emphasis added*

In this story the Lord Himself declared that nothing is impossible to a group of people when they are unified, which can be very exciting or very scary depending on what the group of people are wanting to do. In this case, it was a wrong goal and God had to intervene by stopping their ability to communicate with each other. Keep that in mind, good communication produces unity.

So, to be in unity requires that we be of the "same mind" and "speak the same things." Singing together provides the only way possible to obtain instant and complete unity. Unity then qualifies us to receive the Lords blessing and makes everything possible for us.

UNITY WITH DIVERSITY

Unity is not always unison. As a musical term, unison means the same note. In life, unison means doing the exact same thing. In music, we can be in unity, even though we are not singing the same note.

The three parts to music are melody, rhythm, and harmony. I have already explained how important rhythm is to allow us to sing the same thing at the same time. I have also explained how important melody is so we can sing with the same emotional feelings and specific meanings. Now I would like to explain how the third part of music fits into the production of unity.

What makes music sound so rich and beautiful is the third part of music—harmony. A basic understanding of Harmony is music comprised of "notes which enhance the melody." Harmony is based on the natural overtone series.

Here is a great way to understand overtones. All sound is created by vibrations. If you are playing a stringed instrument, you create sound by making the strings vibrate. When a string vibrates, it not only vibrates as a whole string but divides as it vibrates into halves, thirds, and quarters. The divided vibrating string then produces overtone pitches from those vibrations.

The overtone series then gives us the basis for the fundamental musical triad or basic music cord. The criteria for choosing a musical cord is that the melody note must be one of the notes in the cord.

When we compose music for an orchestra or choir, we give different instruments or different vocal parts different notes within the chords. Everyone is in harmony because they are doing one of the notes within the cord being played or sung. In this regard, music shows us how we can be in unity although we are sounding different notes or doing different things in the expression of worship.

In King Jehoshaphat's day, three kingdoms united against the Israelites. Jehoshaphat called together everyone to seek the Lord, and God answered their prayer with a prophetic word promising them victory in the battle. Different groups and individuals responded differently to that promise from God.

> *13 And all Judah stood before the Lord, with their little ones, their wives, and their children. 18 And Jehoshaphat **bowed** his head with his face to the ground: and all Judah and the inhabitants of Jerusalem **fell** before the Lord, **worshipping** the Lord. 19 And the Levites, of the children of the Kohathites, and of the children of the Korhites, **stood** up to **praise** the Lord God of Israel with a **loud voice** on high.*
> 2 Chronicles 20:13,18-19 (KJV) emphasis added

Within the same congregation we see three different responses to God's promise. They did not have to express themselves in unison to display their unity before God. Likewise, we do not have to sing the same notes when we worship to be in harmony. If we follow the leading of the Holy Spirit, He will orchestrate our worship responses to Him so they are in harmony. Likewise, when we sing with the Spirit, He harmonizes our voices into a spontaneous yet beautiful, harmonious choir.

THE POWER OF MUSIC

Music can originate in and transcend to the human spirit. When I sing with my spirit, and you receive my song into your spirit, you are also receiving any spirit that my spirit is joined to. Whenever I sing, because my spirit is joined to God's Spirit, I am imparting His Spirit to whomever is listening to me. This will happen even if your spirit has not been joined to God's Spirit yet. You will encounter the presence of God when I sing, if I sing with my spirit. However, the effects of His presence will be temporary for you. The length of time God's presence will stay with you will be up to you. If you make Him welcome, He will stay longer.

It works the same way when listening to someone who has joined their spirit to an evil spirit. They will impart to their listeners the presence of that spirit. However, that devil will stay with those listeners because he is a legalist. The Holy Spirit is a gentleman, and will not stay where He's not welcome. The devil is a legalist. If you have listened to his music, that gives him the legal right to stay with you, especially if you keep listening to his music. If you listen to that kind of music enough, you will become controlled by the demons that control the artists and songwriters you are listening to.

This is what makes music so powerful—it is capable of imparting to the listener the same spirit found in the performer and songwriter.

As far back as the 60s, Christians have been trying to figure out what is wrong with certain types of music. Bill Gothard told everybody it was the rhythm part of music that was bad. The problem with that theory is that rhythm is one third of all music. In other words, you cannot have music without rhythm. Others have told us that certain chord progressions are demonic. I have also heard someone say that all music done in a minor key is demonic. None of that is correct. It is the spirit behind the music that defines if the music is bad or not.

My recommendation is for you only to listen to music by songwriters and performers who have joined their spirits to the Holy Spirit. This way you will always be feeding yourself the presence of God!

CHAPTER TWO

"PERFECTED PRAISE"

For more on the topic of "Perfected Praise" read *Biblical Worship.*

SECULAR IDEAS OF PERFECTED PRAISE

What is "perfected praise?" What about our praise and worship qualifies it to be called perfect? Whose standards should we use when we are determining if our praise and worship has been perfected?

In 1982 the Spirit of God told me that it was time to be established in a local setting so I could learn more about worship from Him. To obey His leading, I accepted a position as director of music at the Full Gospel Bible Institute (FGBI) in Eston, Saskatchewan, Canada. This is the official Bible college for the Apostolic Church of Pentecost (ACOP), a Canadian denomination.

The FGBI choir which I directed had fifty or more voices in it. Each year our choir entered the provincial music festival, which was always adjudicated by Canada's top musicians affiliated with the Toronto Conservatory of Music. When the choir participated in the festival in the fall of my second year at FGBI, the adjudicator stopped her judging schedule long enough to follow me out into the hall after we sang our two songs.

"This choir is amazing," she said as she grabbed my arm to stop me. "Where did you get your training?"

"Just at a small university in Kansas," I replied.

"Which university?" she persisted.

"Friends University," I answered, "in Wichita, Kansas."

"Really!" She beamed. "That explains it."

"You've heard of Friends University?"

"You're kidding!" she was shocked. "Everyone in the world in music academia has heard of Friends University."

Secular music training is driven by competition. Everyone is striving to be the best at their instrument or with their voice. It is a badge of honor to be in the first chair position of your instrumental group in your band or orchestra. The best violinist in an orchestra is called the concert master. In a choir the goal is to be the section leader of your vocal part. Every time you participate in a recital or concert, you strive to outshine everyone else who is participating. Secular music training in the highest-level schools is more competitive than most sports.

The most powerful expression of group worship is music; however, when worship musicians have been trained in the secular schools, this spirit or attitude of competition and performance pervades because that's all that has been modeled for us in our training.

This lack of spiritual depth in our worship team members results in a wrong perception as to what perfected praise is. Here are some of the more popular ideas today's worship teams have about what makes praise perfect.

1. Use Only the Best Singers and Players

Once I realized that perfected praise had nothing to do with how well the singers sing and the instrumentalists play, I was able to encourage everyone to worship the Lord no matter how they sound. God does not receive a beautifully trained singer's worship more than He does an untrained or inexperienced singer's worship. God is more concerned about the sound of your heart than the sound of your voice or instrument.

> *But the Lord said unto Samuel, Look not on his countenance, or on the height of his stature; because I have refused him: for the Lord seeth not as man seeth; for man looketh on the outward appearance, but the Lord looketh on the heart. 1 Samuel 16:7 (KJV)*

2. Use Only the Latest Songs

Exposure to radio programming has taught us that songs have a shelf-life, and the best songs are the new songs. Again, this criterion comes from the same spirit of competition which drives secular music training yet is complexed by the greed of the music industry. The criteria for choosing worship music should never be the song's age but whether the Spirit of God rests upon the song, which we call being anointed. We will discuss more about choosing songs for worship in the next book of this series, *Leading Worship*.

3.   Secure the Best Trained, Skillful Leadership

Believe me when I say that your worship leader(s) should be well-trained in every aspect of music, especially in directing large instrumental and choral ensembles. Worship leaders also need to be equipped spiritually to hear from God.

We will further discuss the Biblical qualifications of a worship leader in *Leading Worship*, but please recognize that even if your worship leader(s) meet the criteria, that has nothing to do with what the Bible calls perfected praise.

JESUS' PERFECTED PRAISE

The term "perfected praise" was coined by Jesus Himself in this scripture:

> . . . *and said to Him, "Do You hear what these are saying?"*
> *And Jesus said to them, "Yes. Have you never read, 'Out of the mouth of babes and nursing infants You have **perfected praise**'?" Matthew 21:16 (NKJV) emphasis added*

To fully understand Jesus' meaning of perfected praise, we need to go back in the story just a little. Matthew chapter 21 starts with Jesus' "triumphal entry" on a donkey into Jerusalem, a ride undertaken to fulfill this verse in scripture.

> *Rejoice greatly, O daughter of Zion; shout, O daughter of Jerusalem: behold, thy King cometh unto thee: He is just, and*

having salvation; lowly, and riding upon an ass, and upon a colt the foal of an ass. Zechariah 9:9 (KJV)

This event is the beginning of what is known in church history and on the church calendar as Holy Week. That week in history is a demonstration of how quickly people in power can influence the masses to do what they want them to do.

Jesus' public ministry only lasted about three years; however, because of the fantastic miracles He performed, His fame spread throughout that region. Everywhere Jesus went He drew large crowds. Almost everyone believed that Jesus was the Messiah or Christ sent from God to save His people. Here are a few references that indicate how widespread this belief was during those three years:

Come, see a man, which told me all things that ever I did: is not this the Christ? John 4:29 (KJV)

And said unto the woman, Now we believe, not because of thy saying: for we have heard Him ourselves, and know that this is indeed the Christ, the Savior of the world. John 4:42 (KJV)

But, lo, He speaketh boldly, and they say nothing unto Him. Do the rulers know indeed that this is the very Christ? John 7:26 (KJV)

One of the two which heard John speak, and followed him, was Andrew, Simon Peter's brother. He first findeth his own brother Simon, and saith unto him, We have found the Messias, which is, being interpreted, the Christ. John 1:40-41 (KJV)

But we trusted that it had been He which should have redeemed Israel: and beside all this, today is the third day since these things were done. Luke 24:21 (KJV)

And all the people were amazed, and said, Is not this the Son of David? Matthew 12:23 (KJV)

At that time, the only people who didn't believe that Jesus was the Christ, the Son of David were the religious leaders of the day. Because of that, Jesus had no kind words for them anytime they showed up, as seen in these scriptures.

Woe to you, teachers of the law and Pharisees, you hypocrites! You are like whitewashed tombs, which look beautiful on the outside but on the inside are full of the bones of the dead and everything unclean. Matthew 23:27 (NIV)

O generation of vipers, how can ye, being evil, speak good things? for out of the abundance of the heart the mouth speaketh. Matthew 12:34 (KJV)

So, in a little more than three years many grew to believe that Jesus was the Messiah or Christ who had been prophesied to come to us through the line of David. That is why the large crowd shouted that Jesus was the son of David as He entered the city that day.

*And the multitudes that went before, and that followed, cried, saying, **Hosanna to the son of David**: Blessed is He that cometh in the name of the Lord; Hosanna in the highest. Matthew 21:9 (KJV) emphasis added*

Baker's Evangelical Dictionary of Biblical Theology confirms this:

Those from whose lips "Hosanna" rose that day seem to have looked on Jesus as God's anointed one from the house of David of whom the prophets had spoken and through whom they hoped that all their messianic expectations would be fulfilled.[16]

---

[16] Baker's Evangelical Dictionary of Biblical Theology. Edited by Walter A. Elwell

The next thing that happened in this story is Jesus went to the temple and drove out the money changers. The crowds from the streets pressed into the temple, and many were hoping Jesus would do a miracle for them.

> *And the blind and the lame came to Him in the temple; and He healed them. And when the chief priests and scribes saw the wonderful things that He did, and the children crying in the temple, and saying, Hosanna to the son of David; they were sore displeased, Matthew 21:14-15 (KJV)*

Out on the streets everyone was shouting "Hosanna to the Son of David," but in the temple only the children shouted that declaration. Why? Could it be that the adults had been indoctrinated into the proper religious behavior and knew it was not acceptable to shout in the temple? Or could it be that the adults were more astute at picking up on the moods of other people, and they discerned the religious leaders' disapproval of what had happened in the streets regarding Jesus?

I believe that when Jesus began healing the blind and lame in the temple that day, those children became out-of-control with their excitement. Quite possibly many of them had never seen an actual miracle before but had only heard that Jesus had done miracles in other towns.

Think about it: If you were a kid, and your uncle had not been able to see all your life but now he is looking around, how do you think you would react? You would not be able to contain your excitement even if you wanted to.

Those kids had been taught all their lives that only the Messiah could perform miracles. Now that they had seen Jesus perform them, that could only mean one thing. Jesus is the Christ, the Son of David that everyone has been looking for. This realization added to the children's out-of-control emotional state the way gasoline affects a burning fire.

To try to regain control of their temple, the chief priests and scribes went to Jesus for His help.

> *And said unto Him, Hearest Thou what these say? And Jesus saith unto them, Yea; have ye never read, Out of the mouth of babes and sucklings thou hast perfected praise? Matthew 21:16 (KJV)*

The religious leaders came and pointed out to Jesus that these children were calling Him the Messiah. They wanted Him to tell the children that He was not the Christ. I love Jesus' response to them. Remember, the chief priests' primary responsibility was to read and teach the scriptures. The scribes' primary responsibility was to read and copy the scriptures. Jesus responded to them with a straightforward reply that I've paraphrased as, "Of course I hear what they are saying! What's the matter? Don't you boys ever read the Scriptures?" In that setting, sarcasm was the most appropriate response Jesus could give.

Jesus was saying that perfected praise occurs when we worship Him the way those children did that day in the temple—out-of-control, totally abandoned to joy, noisy, reckless, energetic, and with no regard to religious or political correctness.

Perfected praise is reckless abandonment in our worship as demonstrated for us by these "noisy" children. Perfected praise is simply losing ourselves in the expression of our love of God. Perfected praise is high-energy praise. Perfected praise is highly intensive praise. Perfected praise is acting like an excited, joyful, out-of-control kid.

In *Biblical Worship* I gave the definitions of the Hebrew word *halal*, which is translated into praise in English. The meanings of this word help us understand the type of praise that is acceptable to God. Here is the definition of halal:

1. to shine or give light
2. to be clear (of sound or color)
3. to sing (praises)
4. to celebrate
5. to make a show
6. to boast or be boastful
7. to commend
8. to rave
9. to rage
10. to act like a madman
11. to be clamorously foolish while giving glory[17]

---

[17] Biblical Worship, pages 51-60

This definition of praise sure sounds like what Jesus called perfected praise to me, especially definitions eight through eleven. So, tell me, do those definitions describe your praise of the Lord Jesus? If it doesn't, then I would suggest you're not giving Him perfected praise.

> *Yet you have not called on Me, Jacob, you have not wearied yourselves for Me, Israel. Isaiah 43:22 (NIV)*

Perfected praise is the giving of every ounce of energy we have in worshiping the Lord. This is also confirmed in what is known as the greatest commandment in the Bible.

> *And thou shalt love the Lord thy God with all thine heart, and with all thy soul, and with **all thy might**. Deuteronomy 6:5 (KJV) emphasis added*

ORDAINED STRENGTH

If you do a search, you will discover Matthew 21:16 is the only place in scripture where this phrase perfected praise appears. To the natural mind this presents us with a problem because Jesus quoted an Old Testament scripture. He even prefaced His quote by asking the religious leaders if they could remember reading the scripture He quoted. Here is the scripture Jesus was quoting that day.

> *Out of the mouth of babes and nursing infants You have ordained strength, because of Your enemies, That You may silence the enemy and the avenger. Psalm 8:2 (NKJV)*

The translation of David's psalm reads *"You have ordained strength."* But when Jesus quoted it, He said *"You have perfected praise."* Jesus did not make a mistake. Jesus did not forget what that scripture says and make up something in the moment. Jesus was giving us further insight as to what the Holy Spirit meant in Psalm 8:2. In the kingdom of God, the way God has ordained that you and I would receive strength on this earth is by us spending every ounce of our strength or might in expressing our love to Jesus, like those children did in the temple.

Many times I've worked hard all day and shown up at church for special meetings exhausted and wishing I could just "veg" at home with my feet up while watching a movie. However, Jesus is worthy of my praise and I had committed to worship with my fellow Christians, so I assembled with them and stood up, and offered the sacrifice of praise[18] to the Lord. In those times, if I was conservative with my energy when I worshiped, I always left those meetings more exhausted than when I came. However, if I purposed to abandon myself in worship and use every ounce of energy I had to glorify the Lord, I always left those meetings totally refreshed and with my strength completely renewed.

> *Even the youths shall faint and be weary, and the young men shall utterly fall, but those who wait on the Lord shall renew their strength; they shall mount up with wings like eagles, they shall run and not be weary, they shall walk and not faint. Isaiah 40:30-31 (NKJV)*

It is a mystery to the natural mind how we can receive strength in our bodies by giving the Lord praise with all the strength we have—reckless abandonment to Jesus. But that's the way God has ordained for us to be refreshed according to Jesus.

The world says, "Conserve what energy you have."

The Lord says, "Love me with all your strength!"[19]

The world says, "Conserve what money you have."

The Lord says, "Give and it shall be given unto you."[20]

The wisdom of the kingdom of God is the complete opposite of the wisdom of the flesh and the world, and the two can never coexist. They are enemies of each other!

The big question which now arises is why did God ordain strength for us through our radical praise of Him? The answer to this question is found in Psalm 8:2.

---

[18] Hebrews 13:15, Romans 12:1

[19] Deuteronomy 6:5

[20] Luke 6:38

> *Out of the mouth of babes and nursing infants You have ordained strength, because of Your enemies, That You may* **silence the enemy** *and the avenger. Psalm 8:2 (NKJV) emphasis added*

God wants us to radically praise Him because God has enemies. By our radical praise of Almighty God, He shuts the mouths of His enemy.

WHAT DOES IT MEAN TO SILENCE THE ENEMY?

What does it mean to shut the mouth of the enemy? To fully understand the answer to this question you must remember these concepts I established for you in *Portrait of a Worshiper*.

Make sure you read that book for a more complete understanding of this list.

1. Mankind is created in three parts: spirit, soul, and body.
2. Sin brought death to all three parts.
3. Jesus purchased our entire being back to Himself.
4. A Christian's spirit is joined to God's Spirit.
5. Our soul is not yet saved or delivered but is being renewed in this present life.
6. Our body will be saved in the future.
7. The three tenses of salvation are: the spirit (the past), the soul (the present), and the body (the future).
8. We were created like God in two ways: in God's image and likeness.
9. The likeness of God refers to God's form. God made our form or body like His form.
10. The image of God refers to God's character. Character is the motivation and rationale for our choices

We were made in three parts: spirit, soul, and body.[21] As Christians, our spirit is the only part of us that is saved or delivered on this earth, and it can never be more saved or delivered than it is right now. Our soul is

---

[21] 1 Thessalonians 5:23

undergoing the process of salvation while we are on this earth, which is the specific time God has set up for that process. We call this the "renewing of our mind."[22] Our body will be changed when Jesus returns for us on the day of adoption.[23]

God's enemy, Satan cannot attack God directly because he is no match for God! Therefore, he attacks mankind in our two parts that are not yet redeemed. We were created in God's likeness and image.[24] Satan attacks God's likeness by attacking our bodies. Satan attacks God's image by attacking our souls. Satan attacks our bodies with sickness, disease, and physical calamities. Satan attacks our souls with implanted thoughts and unholy desires and feelings. The soul and the body are vulnerable to Satan's attacks since they are the unredeemed parts of Christians.

It is easily understood how the enemy attacks our bodies with diseases and accidents. What most Christians do not understand is the full extent of the enemy's attacks against our souls. Remember, the enemy's warfare against our soul is done with thoughts, words, and feelings. To stop these types of attacks we must silence the enemy.

Why is it important to silence the enemy? Because he is always talking, he never shuts up! He wants to influence how we think and feel about everything, because he knows that what we think and feel determines everything in our life.

> For **as he thinks** in his heart, **so is he**. "Eat and drink!"
> he says to you, But his heart is not with you. Proverbs 23:7
> (NKJV) emphasis added

The principle is this: Whatever you think, if you think about it long enough, it will happen.

Over the years, many non-Christians have discovered that the truth of this verse works with or without God's involvement in your life. This is simply one of the universal laws that God set up when He made the universe.

Norman Vincent Peale called this *The Power of Positive Thinking*.

---

[22] Romans 12:2

[23] Romans 8:23

[24] Genesis 1:26

Kevin Trudeau and several others call it the Law of Attraction. One secret society calls it the Ten Second Miracle. Every secret society has this as one of their secrets—you get what you think about, positive or negative. Some Christians call this "name it and claim it" or positive confession because of scriptures like this:

> *A good man out of the good treasure of his heart brings forth good; and an evil man out of the evil treasure of his heart brings forth evil. For out of the abundance of the heart his mouth speaks. Luke 6:45 (NKJV)*

In other words, whatever you think about a lot you will talk about a lot. Therefore, what you think about and talk about will many times materialize in your life. This is the principle the Faith Movement of the 1980s was established on. However, it did not always work because some failed to understand the importance of our emotions in the mix. This part of the principle is disguised in the second part of the verse we read earlier.

> *"Eat and drink!" he says to you, But his heart is not with you. Proverbs 23:7b (NKJV)*

Here King Solomon is saying that you can go over to someone's house for supper, but you can tell through their emotions if they really want you there or not. In other words, you can cancel out this principle of thinking and speaking positively or negatively if your heart and emotions are not affected properly by what you are thinking or confessing. Many Christians left the Faith Movement because this aspect of this principle was misunderstood.

Satan knows the power of this universal law, so whenever he attacks us, he never just hits our bodies. The second of his "one-two punches" is always to the mind and emotions. If he can get you to believe that his attack on your body is serious, it will be. If he can get you to think that his attack on your body is severe enough to take you out, it will. If you think when calamity comes that your God is capable of saving you, no matter what, then He will. It is in the battleground of the mind that we win or lose our battles with the enemy. That is why he must be silenced.

There is a true story that demonstrates how God moves and overrides the physical realm when someone aligns their words and thoughts with their passion or emotions.

In October 2014 my friend Lee Birch was working in a factory as a maintenance man. One day he was working on the motor of a Genie lift bucket vehicle whose base weighed 9,000 pounds. The engine was running but not in gear, yet out of nowhere the vehicle engaged and began moving out of the shop. When Lee ran after it, his pants got caught, and the lift rolled on top of him. It high-centered with the entire weight of the vehicle directly on his chest.

It took fifteen minutes for a heavy forklift to remove that piece of equipment from Lee's body. He was dead—and blue. The EMT could find no pulse and no sign of life.

A Mennonite coworker knelt beside Lee, moved by compassion from the stories Lee had told him of his many mission trips to Haiti and the orphanage Lee and his wife sponsor there.

"Lord, he can't die," the coworker prayed. "The kids in Haiti need him." He stared at Lee's lifeless body for a sign that his prayer had been answered, but nothing happened.

Broken to the point of tears, the coworker slumped over with his mouth near Lee's ear. Quietly, yet in desperation, he spoke. "Lee Birch, in the name of Jesus, you come back to life!"

"We have a pulse!" the EMT shouted.

Lee was flown by helicopter to the St. Francis Hospital in Wichita, Kansas. After being checked out by the trauma and critical injury teams, it was pronounced that Lee had no broken bones, internal injuries, or bleeding. When his wife arrived at the hospital, he was sitting up on the hospital bed and talking to everybody. Since the doctors and nurses couldn't find anything wrong, they let him go home.

I am describing how the natural laws in Lee's case were overridden by the spiritual law of faith. It is also what happened to me.

In the preface of this book I shared my trauma story of being shot. My thoughts throughout that ordeal were based on the words the Lord spoke to me right after it happened, that everything would be all right. I joined my emotions to those words by simply yielding to the peace of God as I waited for God's promise to play itself out. Just like in Lee's case, natural laws were overridden by the spiritual law of faith.

Another friend named Cliff Brown was diagnosed with metastatic stage-four cancer more than seven years ago. He was supposed to die within weeks of that initial diagnosis but worked in a factory job most of the last few years. He did not fear the cancer, so the cancer did not kill him (*as he thinks . . . so is he*) when it was supposed to. Recently he did pass over to be with Jesus, after he told me he would be going soon, because it was time. Doctors still have no explanation for his lengthy survival.

The difference is made in what someone thinks or speaks and how they feel about what they think or speak. In mine and Cliff's cases, we had a word from God we focused on.

Satan knows how this works, which is why he tries to shape the thoughts and feelings in every person he is attacking, so his attack will be successful. That is why God has provided a way for us to silence the enemy. Without the thoughts and feelings Satan gives us, his attacks against us are powerless!

Again, how does God silence the enemy and provide us with strength? Through perfected praise. Radical, exuberant praise silences the enemy so he cannot lie to us. Total abandonment, raging praise keeps the enemy's lying mouth shut. What an amazing spiritual warfare tool that God has given to us.

Why is it important to shut the enemy up, thereby stopping the lies before Satan feeds them to us? Because, once a thought has entered our mind, it takes much more energy to battle that thought in our mind than it does to worship God with "perfected praise," and keep the thought from entering our mind in the first place.

HOW DID LUCIFER BECOME THE ENEMY OF GOD?

Before he was called Satan or the devil, in heaven he was called Lucifer. God, through Isaiah tells us what happened.

> *How art thou fallen from heaven, O Lucifer, son of the morning! how art thou cut down to the ground, which didst weaken the nations! For thou hast said in thine heart, **I will ascend** into heaven, I will exalt my throne above the stars*

*of God: I will sit also upon the mount of the congregation, in the sides of the north: I will ascend above the heights of the clouds; **I will be like the most High**. Yet thou shalt be brought down to hell, to the sides of the pit. Isaiah 14:12-15 (KJV) emphasis added*

Lucifer committed two grave sins: The first was when he said, "I will ascend," and the second was wanting to be like God. There are five places listed where he wanted to ascend.

1. into heaven
2. above the stars of God
3. the mount of the congregation
4. the sides of the north
5. above the heights of the clouds

All these places are reserved for the Lord God only. They are the places that set God apart from every created being and show He is worthy of praise from all His creation. By wanting to ascend to these places, Lucifer was saying that he wanted to receive worship for himself and take it away from God.

Lucifer's second sin was that he wanted to be like God. He could not accept himself the way God made him. He was not satisfied with the way he looked nor with the purpose for which God assigned him. Lucifer wanted to look and be like God, and he wanted to receive worship for himself.

LUCIFER'S FIRST PUNISHMENT FOR THESE SINS

The scripture we read in Isaiah 14 begins with the first part of Lucifer's punishment.

How art thou fallen from heaven, O Lucifer, son of the morning! how art thou cut down to the ground, which didst weaken the nations! Isaiah 14:12 (KJV)

Fallen from heaven could indicate an accident happened, but when put together with *cut down to the ground*, it becomes clear that Lucifer ended up on the ground because someone with authority over him put him there.

We know from scripture that Lucifer was one of three archangels in heaven. The two other Archangels mentioned in the Bible are Gabriel (Head of Communications), and Michael (the General over the Angel Armies). Lucifer's position was heavenly worship leader. We will discuss this in detail in the next book of this series, *Leading Worship*.

The Bible makes it clear that an Archangels have the highest rank among angels in their chain-of-command, so only God outranks them. From this knowledge we understand that God threw Lucifer out of heaven as his first punishment. This judgment action was swift and decisive, as witnessed by Jesus:

> *And he said unto them, I beheld Satan as lightning fall*
> *from heaven. Luke 10:18 (KJV)*

Where did God banish Lucifer to? Isaiah told us Lucifer was *cut down to the ground*.[25] According to Strong's Concordance, the English word "ground" is the Hebrew word Number 0776, which is 'erets (eh'-rets)[26]. This Hebrew word is translated as "land" 1,543 times, "earth" 712 times, "ground" ninety-eight times, and "world" four times. Lucifer, then, was banished to the earth, the same place God created and placed man.

If God had asked my opinion about that idea, I would have suggested He banish Lucifer to a different place than where He put mankind. Of course, God didn't ask me about that. As a matter of fact, mankind wasn't even in existence when Lucifer was kicked out of heaven.

LUCIFER'S SECOND PUNISHMENT

So why did God put mankind on earth where He banished Satan? The answer is found in this scripture verse.

> *Let the saints be joyful in glory: let them sing aloud upon*
> *their beds. Let the high praises of God be in their mouth, and*

---

[25] Isaiah 14:12

[26] Strong's Concordance

a two edged sword in their hand; To execute vengeance upon
the heathen, and punishments upon the people; To bind their
kings with chains, and their nobles with fetters of iron; To
execute upon them the judgment written: this honor have all
His saints. Praise ye the LORD. Psalm 149:5-9 (KJV)

Here are some of the instructions given to us in this verse:

1. Be joyful while giving God glory.

God wants praise and worship, which comes out of a joyful heart. Getting that excited about giving God glory fits the description of perfected praise.

2. Sing our praise to God aloud.

We should sing loud praises to God in places where normally we would not be loud, such as in the temple or on our beds.

3. Let high praises be in our mouth, which is a two-edged sword in our hand.

The phrase *high praises* does not occur anywhere else in scripture. In the context of this chapter where we have just been commanded to be joyful while giving glory and to sing loudly in places we are expected to be quiet, high praises are the same thing that Jesus called perfected praise—reckless abandonment, clamorously foolish worship.

I first introduced Hebrew Parallelism, the eastern hemisphere's writing technique of saying the same thing in two different ways, in *Biblical Worship*.[27] Several examples of parallelism from scripture are highlighted in chapter 8 of that book. In Psalm 149:6, there's another example of parallelism:

Let the high praises of God be in their mouth, and a two-
edged sword in their hand; Psalm 149:6 (KJV)

Parallelism is the forerunner of the English metaphor, and in this case, it is exactly the same. What is being said here is that "high" energy "praise" in our mouth is the same thing as a two-edged sword in our hand in the spiritual realm. Paul confirms this for us in his letter to the Ephesians.

---

[27] Stone, S. *Biblical Worship.* 2012. Nashville, TN: Westbow Press.

And take . . . the sword of the Spirit . . . Ephesians 6:17 (KJV)

Why would God make our praise equivalent to a spiritual sword and strong chains? And who are these weapons to be used against? The answer to these questions is found in verses seven through nine of Psalm 149.

Psalm 149: Worshipers' Responsibilities

What Are We to Do?	To Whom Are We to Do It?
Execute vengeance	*upon the heathen*
(Execute) punishments	*upon the people*
Bind with chains	*their kings*
(Bind) with fetters of iron	*their nobles*
Execute the judgment written	*upon them* (all of the above)

Table IX

Most theologians agree that the composer of this psalm is not talking about natural people, kings, and nobles but rather the spiritual hierarchy of the demonic realm. Even Paul referred to this satanic chain of command in his letter to the Ephesians when he outlined who Christians battle.

> *Finally, my brethren, be strong in the Lord, and in the power of his might. Put on the whole armour of God, that ye may be able to stand against the wiles of the devil. For we wrestle not against flesh and blood, but against principalities, against powers, against the rulers of the darkness of this world, against spiritual wickedness in high places. Ephesians 6:10-12 (KJV)*

I find it interesting to compare these verses.

Demonic Chain of Command

Psalm 149:7–9	Eph 6:10–12
upon the heathen	principalities
upon the people	powers

their kings	rulers of the darkness
their nobles	spiritual wickedness in high places

Table X

Notice that the conflict we are in is not a physical battle against people despite that our enemy likes to influence and use other people to attack us.

> *For we wrestle not against flesh and blood . . . Ephesians 6:12 (KJV)*

Not only can people be used innocently by the devil to attack us, but we can also be used against our will by a demon to attack someone else. This happened to Peter when Jesus asked the disciples who men were saying that He was. After the disciples told Jesus their answers, He asked them who they thought He was. Peter answered quickly that Jesus was the Christ. Jesus commended Peter for receiving that revelation from the Spirit of God. Then a few minutes later when Jesus was trying to prepare His disciples for how He would die on the cross and be resurrected, Peter reacted out of his natural love for Jesus.

> *Then Peter took Him, and began to rebuke Him, saying, Be it far from thee, Lord: this shall not be unto thee. But He (Jesus) turned, and said unto Peter, Get thee behind me, Satan: thou art an offence unto Me: for thou savourest not the things that be of God, but those that be of men. Matthew 16:22-23 (KJV)*

If Peter could fall prey to being used by the devil against Jesus just moments after he received the greatest spiritual revelation of his life, then we also have the potential of being used in the same way against our brothers and sisters in Christ. Notice the qualification to be used of the devil in attacking someone else is not to savor the things of the devil but rather to savor the things of men over the things of God. That means all of us will qualify for being used by the devil many times every day. Sometimes Satan takes advantage of us, and sometimes he misses the opportunity.

If the enemy can get us to attack each other with his thoughts and feelings rather than attack the evil hierarchy Paul has listed for us, then the enemy will have succeeded with one of his favorite tactics of warfare. Joined with this style of spiritual attack from the enemy is Satan's convincing us not to forgive our fellow man so he can keep things stirred up between us and remain in the background undetected.

Since we are not fighting in the natural realm, the weapons we use in this warfare come from the Spirit of God, like He gives us spiritual gifts.

> *(For the weapons of our warfare are not carnal, but mighty through God to the pulling down of strong holds;) 2 Corinthians 10:4 (KJV)*

You cannot use natural weapons to fight a spiritual war. However, all spiritual weapons have a natural component to them. All spiritual weapons depend on our obedience to be effective.

THIS IS OUR HONOR

The list of responsibilities in Psalm 149 is followed by this sentence.

> *. . . this honor have **all His** saints. Praise ye the LORD. Psalm 149:9 (KJV) emphasis added*

If you are a Christian, if you are one of God's saints made righteous by the blood of Jesus, then it is your honor to carry out God's judgment against His enemies with your worship of God.

Lucifer wanted to be like God, so as part of his punishment, God made mankind in His own likeness and image to remind Lucifer that he will never be like God. Lucifer wanted to receive worship, so as part of his punishment, God made mankind's primary purpose to be worshipers of the Most High. Plus, God made mankind's worship of Him to be as painful as a sword and as debilitating as chains and fetters to Lucifer and all his followers.

God did not put mankind on the earth to be tormented by the devil but rather God put mankind on the earth to punish the devil! We carry out God's judgment against the devil every time we worship God with perfected praise.

CHAPTER THREE

"THE POWER OF WORSHIPING TOGETHER"

THE CONFLICT

God banished Lucifer to earth where He created mankind to punish Lucifer with worship of Himself. Lucifer is bound when God's saints give Him high praises, which means Satan (formerly Lucifer) is not bound when we don't function the way God designed us to function as worshipers.

When Lucifer is bound, he cannot affect any harm on God's people or anyone near God's worshipers; however, when Satan is not being bound through our worship, he is free to go on the offensive. I'm sure you have heard that the best defense is a good offence. Satan knows that and applies it every chance he gets.

Worship is not something to make us feel good. Worship is survival. Worship is life and death to God's people. Satan knows we were created to punish him with our worship, and he will do everything in his power to keep us from worshiping God.

SPIRITUAL WARFARE

Spiritual warfare is just that—a conflict carried on in the spiritual realm, not the physical realm. The enemy, however, wants us to think we are fighting a physical battle so he can defeat us. We are no match for the devil in the physical realm. Martin Luther understood that and wrote about it in his great hymn "A Mighty Fortress Is Our God." Please take the time to read all his lyrics since only the first four verses appear in most hymnals.

A Mighty Fortress Is Our God (Ein Feste Burg)
Written by Martin Luther in 1529
Translated into English by Frederick H. Hedge in 1853

Verse 1
A mighty fortress is our God
A bulwark never failing
Our helper He amid the flood
Of mortal ills prevailing
For still our ancient foe
Doth seek to work us woe
His craft and pow'r are great
And armed with cruel hate
On earth is not his equal

Verse 2
Did we in our own strength confide
Our striving would be losing
Were not the right Man on our side
The Man of God's own choosing
Dost ask who that may be
Christ Jesus it is He
Lord Sabaoth His name
From age to age the same
And He must win the battle

Verse 3
And tho' this world with devils filled
Should threaten to undo us
We will not fear for God hath willed
His truth to triumph thru us
The prince of darkness grim
We tremble not for him

His rage we can endure
For lo his doom is sure
One little word shall fell him

Verse 4
That word above all earthly pow'rs
No thanks to them abideth
The Spirit and the gifts are ours
Thru Him who with us sideth
Let goods and kindred go
This mortal life also
The body they may kill
God's truth abideth still
His kingdom is forever

Verse 5
A mighty fortress is our God
A sword and shield victorious
He breaks the cruel oppressor's rod
And wins salvation glorious
The old satanic foe
Has sworn to work us woe
With craft and dreadful might
He arms himself to fight
On earth he has no equal

Verse 6
No strength of ours can match his might
We would be lost rejected
But now a champion comes to fight
Whom God Himself elected
You ask who this may be
The Lord of hosts is He
Christ Jesus mighty Lord
God's only Son adored
He holds the field victorious

Verse 7
Though hordes of devils fill the land
All threat'ning to devour us
We tremble not unmoved we stand
They cannot overpow'r us
Let this world's tyrant rage
In battle we'll engage
His might is doomed to fail
God's judgment must prevail
One little word subdues him

Verse 8
God's Word forever shall abide
No thanks to foes who fear it
For God Himself fights by our side
With weapons of the Spirit
Were they to take our house
Goods honor child or spouse
Though life be wrenched away
They cannot win the day
The Kingdom's ours forever

Verse 9
A mighty fortress is our God
A trusty shield and weapon
He helps us free from ev'ry need
That hath us now o'ertaken
The old evil foe
Now means deadly woe
Deep guile and great might
Are his dread arms in fight
On earth is not his equal

Verse 10
With might of ours can naught be done
Soon were our loss effected

But for us fights the valiant One
Whom God Himself elected
Ask ye Who is this
Jesus Christ it is
of sabaoth Lord
And there's none other God
He holds the field forever

Verse 11
Though devils all the world should fill
All eager to devour us
We tremble not we fear no ill
They shall not overpow'r us
This world's prince may still
Scowl fierce as he will
He can harm us none
He's judged the deed is done
One little word can fell him

Verse 12
The Word they still shall let remain
Nor any thanks have for it
He's by our side upon the plain
With His good gifts and Spirit
And take they our life
Goods fame child and wife
Though these all be gone
Our vict'ry has been won
The Kingdom ours remaineth[28]

It is my belief that every line of this hymn contains great wisdom concerning spiritual warfare. Here are a few of of the important concepts found in this song:

---

[28] A Mighty Fortress © Words and music: Public Domain

Martin Luther on Spiritual Warfare

From Martin Luther	My Comments
For still our ancient foe Doth seek to work us woe	Satan is God's enemy; however, since God made us to avenge Him, Satan is our enemy as well.
His craft and pow'r are great And armed with cruel hate	Satan is crafty and powerful and is motivated by his all-consuming hatred of God and those created in God's image.
On earth is not his equal	No human is capable of standing up to Satan's attacks on their own strength and merit.
And tho' this world with devils filled Should threaten to undo us	There are a lot of devils in this world trying to stop us from offering God high praises.
We will not fear for God hath willed His **truth** to triumph thru us	It is of utmost importance for us to not fear the enemy. The victory in the battle between God and Satan will be won through us offering God high praises.
His rage we can endure For lo his doom is sure One little word shall fell him	One little word, the name of Jesus spoken or sung in high praises, will knock Satan back and down.
The Spirit and the gifts are ours	The baptism of the Holy Spirit and the gifts of the Holy Spirit are very important in this battle.
Let this world's tyrant rage In battle we'll engage	God has always intended for us to be involved in this fight against His enemy.
For God Himself fights by our side With weapons of the Spirit	*(For the weapons of our warfare are not carnal, but mighty through God to the pulling down of strong holds;)* 2 Corinthians 10:4 (KJV)
But for us fights the valiant One Whom God Himself elected	Jesus fights for us by fighting through us with spiritual weapons.

Ask ye Who is this Jesus Christ it is of sabaoth Lord And there's none other God	Jesus is the true and living God, the creator of all that exists. He is not just the Son of God; He is God Himself come in the flesh.
Though devils all the world should fill All eager to devour us	This is a dangerous battle with an enemy who wants to devour us, not just hinder us.
He's judged the deed is done	Satan has been judged by the Righteous Judge, and these judgments have been written down in Isaiah chapter 14. The saints are responsible for and honored to execute these judgments.
He's by our side upon the plain With His good gifts and Spirit	We are not on our own in executing these judgments. We have both Christ's in-dwelling Spirit and His gifts, which makes all the difference in the battle.

Table XI

THE WEAPONS OF OUR WARFARE

The term weapons of our warfare comes from this verse:

> *For though we walk in the flesh, we do not war after the flesh: (For the weapons of our warfare are not carnal, but mighty through God to the pulling down of strong holds;) 2 Corinthians 10:3-4 (KJV)*

In Ephesians chapter 6 Paul lists the spiritual armor God has provided for us to fight with in our spiritual warfare against the enemy.

> *Therefore take up the **whole armor** of God, that you may be able to withstand in the evil day, and having done all, to stand. Stand therefore, having **girded your waist** with truth, having put on the **breastplate** of righteousness,*

*and having **shod your feet** with the preparation of the gospel of peace; above all, taking the **shield** of faith with which you will be able to quench all the fiery darts of the wicked one. And take the **helmet** of salvation, and the **sword** of the Spirit, which is the word of God; Ephesians 6:13-17 (NKJV) emphasis added*

The whole armor is made up of these parts:

The Armor of God

Armor Pieces	Spiritual Counterpart
Girded waist	Truth
Breastplate	Righteousness
Shod feet	Prepared Gospel of peace
Shield	Faith
Helmet	Salvation
Sword	Word of God

Table XII

All of these pieces of armor are for our protection or defense except one: the sword. Therefore, the only weapon designed for attacking an enemy is the sword.

To my knowledge, we have been given only two offensive weapons to be used in spiritual warfare, and both are said to "be" swords.

1. High praises

    Let the high praises of God be in their mouth, and a two edged sword in their hand; Psalm 149:6 (KJV)

For an example of praise being effective in spiritual warfare we can look at David and Saul in the Old Testament.

And it came to pass, when the evil spirit from God was upon Saul, that David took an harp, and played with his hand: so Saul was refreshed, and was well, and the evil spirit departed from him. 1 Samuel 16:23 (KJV)

It would appear that David was able to chase away the evil spirit from Saul by simply playing one of his psalms, which praise God.

The one drawback with this particular spiritual weapon is that when you stop praising God, the evil spirits eventually return, as they did to Saul. Our high praises only temporarily affect our enemy. As long as we are worshiping God with high praise, our enemy is bound and held at bay with that spiritual sword. Only the sword of the Word of Truth can deliver lasting deliverance in a person's life.

2. The Word of God

The second spiritual sword mentioned in the Bible is the truth of God's Word.

> *And take the helmet of salvation, and the **sword** of the Spirit, which is the **word** of God . . . Ephesians 6:17 (KJV) emphasis added*

> *For the **word** of God is quick, and powerful, and sharper than any two-edged **sword**, piercing even to the dividing asunder of soul and spirit, and of the joints and marrow, and is a discerner of the thoughts and intents of the heart. Hebrews 4:12 (KJV) emphasis added*

The best example of using the Word of God to defeat the devil comes from when the Spirit led Jesus led into the desert to fast for forty days and afterward the devil attacked Him from three different vantage points. Notice Jesus' response to each of these attacks:

> *But He answered and said, **It is written** . . . Jesus said unto him, **It is written** again . . . Then saith Jesus unto him, Get thee hence, Satan: for **it is written** . . . Matthew 4:4,7,10 (KJV) emphasis added*

Jesus' reaction to each challenge was to declare the truth about each lie (or half-truth) Satan threw at him. It is interesting to me that Jesus, the one with all power and authority, didn't rebuke the devil as many of us seem to do in what we call deliverance sessions.

BIBLICAL DELIVERANCE

Permanent "deliverance" from a demonic attack requires that victims learn and confess the truth about any given lying attack from the enemy, as Jesus did in the example we just looked at. The knowledge of truth is the beginning of deliverance.

> *And ye shall know the truth, and the truth shall make you free. John 8:32 (KJV)*

Most people quote this Scripture incorrectly, which changes its entire meaning. Notice it does not say the truth shall "set" you free but that the truth will "make" you free.

To be set free implies that an instantaneous magical formula has been discovered that will all-of-a-sudden unlock our prison door. To be made free implies a process, not an instantaneous fix. Discovering the truth and rejecting the lies, which are the strongholds the devil has set up in our minds, takes a plodding style of approach. It takes adding line upon line, precept upon precept[29], truth upon truth. It requires the continual washing of the water of the Word,[30] the ongoing renewing of our mind[31].

Biblical deliverance is not some magical moment when someone rebukes the devil away from you. Biblical deliverance is that wonderful moment when you discover the truth from God concerning a particular stronghold that the enemy has held in your mind. Once you have discovered the truth, you can repent for believing that lie and embrace and declare the truth.

> *In meekness instructing those that oppose themselves; if God peradventure will give them **repentance to the acknowledging of the truth**; And that they may recover*

---

[29] Isaiah 28:13
[30] Ephesians 5:26
[31] Romans 12:2

themselves out of the snare of the devil, who are taken captive
by him at his will. 2 Timothy 2:25-26 (KJV)

Deliverance is not someone rebuking the devil away from or out of us. True lasting Biblical deliverance happens when we recover ourselves out of the snare of the devil by repenting for believing a lie and acknowledge the truth about that lie.

Praise drives back the deceptive, demonic forces that have set up strongholds in our minds. High praise allows us a window of opportunity to receive true revelation knowledge from the Word of God concerning the strongholds where we are still in bondage to the demonic realm. Without high praise driving back the deceptive, controlling spirits that have attacked us, we cannot hear and receive the Word of truth.

Every Protestant church has worship by singing and a presentation of the Word of God as their two main components of their gatherings. Even liturgical churches have these two components but add the Eucharist as the third and focal component of their masses. It is not by accident that our church gatherings are structured this way. God has made sure we use the two offensive weapons He has given us when we come together.

It doesn't work to put the Word first. The worship is first so that the demon spirits that have come into church that day, attached to the many strongholds we all have, are driven away so we can receive the Word of God unhindered by the lies of the enemy. Once the stronghold has been destroyed by our repenting for believing a lie and our declaring the Word of Truth, the demons have no more open door to control our thinking from in that particular subject.

Not only does our high praises drive back and chain up the demonic forces attacking us, but it will free up other people in our proximity for a window of time, such as when David's worship freed Saul. This makes it possible for them to hear and understand the Word of Truth without the lies of the devil being fed into their mind to contradict that truth.

Remember, lasting deliverance comes this way. Once we understand the truth, we choose to align ourselves with it by repenting for believing the lie and acknowledging the truth. We do this as often as necessary to establish that truth in our lives.

That process is what James calls submitting to God in his three-step deliverance formula.

> *Submit yourselves therefore to God. Resist the devil, and*
> *he will flee from you. Draw nigh to God, and He will draw*
> *nigh to you. James 4:7-8 (KJV)*

Submitting to God involves these two things.

1. Submitting to His Lordship by offering Him high praises.
2. Submitting to His righteousness by acknowledging His truth.

Once you have submitted to God, you'll have the spiritual and legal right to do steps two and three in James' three-step deliverance formula: resist the devil and draw close to God. If you do not do step one of this process, you will be unsuccessful at step two and three.

Notice that steps two and three have promises attached to them. By doing step one, it qualifies us to do steps two and three and to expect the promised results. In other words, if we don't do step one first, we can't expect the promised results from steps two and three.

James' Deliverance Formula

Step	What We Do	What God Promises
1	Submit to God	(Implied) You can do step two
2	Resist the devil	*he will flee from you*
3	Draw near to God	*He will draw nigh to you*

Table XIII

Often the demons we expel from our lives through James' deliverance formula will return with the same attacks just to see if we really have embraced the truth about their lie or if we will cave in again to their lie. In that case, get out the ole swords once more. With the sword of truth, we resist the devil. With the sword of high praise, we draw near to God. If we meet every spiritual attack in this manner, we have been promised that we will be successful in our spiritual warfare.

Here are some other important concepts concerning deliverance and spiritual warfare taken from this scripture:

In meekness instructing those that oppose themselves; if God peradventure will give them repentance to the acknowledging of the truth; And that they may recover themselves out of the snare of the devil, who are taken captive by him at his will. 2 Timothy 2:25-26 (KJV)

1. Instruct Them in Meekness

The opposite of meekness is pride or anger. These are strongholds from which the enemy uses to control our thinking. Plus, God resists the proud.[32] Why are we to remain meek when helping others?

Brethren, if a man be overtaken in a fault, ye which are spiritual, restore such an one in the spirit of meekness; considering thyself, lest thou also be tempted. Galatians 6:1 (KJV)

The reason we are to remain meek when helping others is because we have the same potential of falling for the devil's lies as anybody else has.

2. Those Who Oppose Themselves

To walk in deception means we're fighting against ourselves because

---

[32] James 4:6

our heart (our spirit) desires truth and the liberty it brings, but the natural mind has been ensnared by a lie.

3. We Must Recover Ourselves

It is the responsibility of the person who has believed a lie or half-truth to recover themselves out of the devil's snare. They cannot take a passive role in this process, waiting on someone else to command their demons to leave them. They must acknowledge the truth that has been revealed to them for themselves, and they must participate in the high praises of God—privately and with others—as a demonstration to God and the demonic realm that they are seeking truth. They must also receive instructions from other Christians who have declared the truth to them. Also, they must be quick to repent when they discover they have believed a lie or half-truth.

JOINING FORCES

We've seen how David, by his praise, chased away the evil spirit that troubled Saul. Logic would tell us that if one worshiper with high praises can chase one evil spirit away, then two worshipers can chase two demons away. Then three demons are chased by three worshipers, and on and on it goes. This is the principle of addition.

God is seldom into addition in scriptures, but He seems to like multiplication much better. When it comes to binding and chasing demons, God has made a covenant promise to us that puts spiritual warfare greatly in our favor.

> *And ye shall chase your enemies, and they shall fall before you by the **sword**. And five of you shall chase an hundred, and an hundred of you shall put ten thousand to flight: and your enemies shall fall before you by the **sword**. For I will have respect unto you, and make you fruitful, and multiply you, and establish **my covenant** with you. Leviticus 26:3-9 (KJV) emphasis added*

Because God has made a covenant with us, He honors it by setting in place this supernatural equation for us to use when dealing with our enemy. He promises that when we come together in unity for the purpose of offering Him high praises, our ability to defeat the enemy will increase exponentially. God's covenant promise to us is that five of us will be able to chase and bind one hundred evil spirits, which means that when we join our hearts together in unity in high praises, five of us will be twenty times more effective than one would be.

With the understanding of this covenant promise, worshiping together suddenly becomes a priority component toward the effectiveness of our spiritual warfare. This would explain why Satan targets Christian unity in worship with such fervor to destroy it and why we should protect our unity in worship at all costs.

The more people who come together in high praises, the more effective our praises are against our enemy. The promise found in

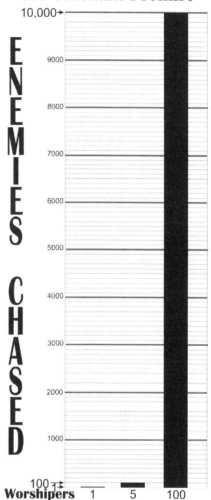

The Effectiveness of Worshiping Together according to *Leviticus 26:3-9*

Leviticus chapter 26 tells us that God exponentially increases His help when we're chasing our enemies. One hundred unified, worshiping saints can put ten thousand demons to flight, which means 100 worshipers are one hundred times more effective than one of us by ourselves.

For those of you who are visual learners like myself I have put together a graph showing this promised exponential curve of effectiveness. God promised us this exponential curve because it is increasingly more and more difficult to assemble higher numbers of worshipers willing to worship with high praises. So, that difficulty is reflected in the reward. In other words, God rewards our overcoming of the temptation not to meet with other worshipers with greater results.

One person can easily fall into deception because demons like to attack in packs. With five people together it becomes a more difficult for the enemy to succeed, but it is still quite probable. But the more people you add into a committed accountability relationship with each other, the less likely deception will occur, and the more effective their praise of God will be and their ability to provide a safe haven for demonized people to encounter the truth, and find true deliverance from spiritual torment.

SPECIAL EXCEPTIONS

These covenant promises we read in Leviticus chapter 26 are the promised proportions of effectiveness that God has put in place for His people when engaged in spiritual warfare together. There are, however, two scripture verses in which God has changed the odds to be profoundly, overwhelmingly in favor of His covenant people, even more so than the guaranteed one hundred times more effective promised in the covenant.

> *For the LORD hath driven out from before you great nations and strong: but as for you, no man hath been able to stand before you unto this day. One man of you shall chase a thousand: for the LORD your God, He it is that fighteth for you, as He hath promised you.*
>
> *Take good heed therefore unto yourselves, that ye love the LORD your God. Else if ye do in any wise go back, and cleave unto the remnant of these nations, even these that remain among you, and shall make marriages with them, and go in unto them, and they to you: Know for a certainty that the LORD your God will no more drive out any of these nations from before you; but they shall be snares and traps unto you, and scourges in your sides, and thorns in your eyes, until ye*

perish from off this good land which the LORD your God hath given you.

And, behold, this day I am going the way of all the earth: and ye know in all your hearts and in all your souls, that not one thing hath failed of all the good things which the LORD your God spake concerning you; all are come to pass unto you, and not one thing hath failed thereof. Joshua 23:9-14 (KJV)

Covenant is unconditional. We keep a covenant because we or our ancestors made the promise, not because the other side kept their promise to us. In this verse, God made a special promise over and above the covenant between He and His people. I say this because of the conditions He outlined for them. If this promise was part of the covenant He made with them, there would be no conditions. This promise includes God fighting for these people in such a way that one of them can be just as effective as twenty normally are in their spiritual warfare. For these reasons it is clear to me that this promise is an exception to the rule, not the rule.

The second instance in Scripture in which the odds change drastically in spiritual warfare also proves why this exception occurs.

How should one chase a thousand, and two put ten thousand to flight, except their rock had sold them, and the LORD had shut them up? For their rock is not as our Rock, even our enemies themselves being judges. Deuteronomy 32:30-31 (KJV)

Rock in this verse refers to a leader that the rank-and-file members follow. Also, when reading this, insert the word "out" after the word "them." Now read it this way.

*"How should one chase a thousand, and two put ten thousand to flight, except their [**leader**] had sold them [**out**], and the LORD had shut them up?" Deuteronomy 32:30 (KJV) paraphrased*

Two things must happen for one of us to chase away 1,000 of our enemies and for two of us to chase away 10,000. Firstly, the leaders of our enemies must sell out their troops, which means they run away from the battle leaving the lower ranking demons to fight on their own. Secondly, the Lord must shut up the mouths of our enemies. When these two things happen, spiritual warfare becomes extremely more effective for us than normal.

Why will the higher-ranking demons run from the battle? Because our unified perfected/high praises have resulted in, *"the LORD had shut them up."*

> *Out of the mouth of babes and nursing infants You have ordained strength, because of Your enemies, That You may* **silence the enemy** *and the avenger. Psalm 8:2 (NKJV) emphasis added*

Perfected praise—radical, out of control rage while praising God—by God's people silences the enemy or shuts their mouths. When we have succeeded at accomplishing that, the higher-ranking demons will usually flee because they know what is coming. At that point our high praises kick us into a completely new dimension of effectiveness.

The Covenant Exception

The Effectiveness of Worship Warfare in *Deuteronomy 32:30*

Then one of us is 1,000 times more effective in spiritual warfare, and two of us are 10,000 times more effective. At that point in this spiritual battle the odds are extremely in our favor if we:

1. Give radical, high perfected praise with as many worshipers as possible as often as possible.
2. Seek to know and embrace God's truth at all costs.

WORSHIP TOGETHER

We have seen that it is more important for us to worship together than it is for us to worship individually. It all has to do with the spiritual warfare in which Christians find ourselves.

While we are worshiping God and focusing on how great our God is, that has a binding and painful effect upon God's enemies. God never intended, however, for us to fight our spiritual warfare on His behalf as individuals, which is why He made our worship together much more effective than our individual worship.

CHAPTER FOUR

"TWO LEVELS OF RELATIONSHIPS"

THE WORSHIP CYCLE

To understand what is happening between us and the Lord when we worship Him, I would like to remind you of the "Worship Cycle"[33].

In Isaiah chapter 6 we learn that every time we worship God, He reveals something about Himself to us. This revelation will result in us being motivated to worship God more, which will result in God revealing more of Himself to us. This cycle is then self-perpetuating for our lifetime and for all of eternity. It will take us an eternity to begin to know God in the ways He wants to reveal Himself to us.

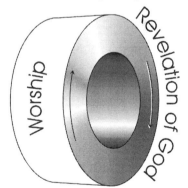

The Worship Cycle

We are describing an eternal, growing relationship with our Creator who is the object of our worship. It is very important to have a developing relationship with the One we are worshiping because there is no worship without a love relationship between God and man.

---

[33] Stone, S. *Biblical Worship*. 2012, Nashville, TN: Westbow Press.

TYPES OF RELATIONSHIPS

The English Christian poet John Donne (1572–1631) published these words in *Devotions Upon Emergent Occasions* in 1624.

No man is an island entire of itself;
Every man is a piece of the continent, a part of the main;
If a clod be washed away by the sea,
Europe is the less, as well as if a promontory were,
As well as any manner of thy friends
Or of thine own were;
Any man's death diminishes me,
Because I am involved in mankind.
And therefore never to know for whom the bell tolls;
It tolls for thee.[34]

Mankind was put on this earth to live and function in two types of relationships. The first type is a relationship with the Creator. This is a special relationship designed by God to allow His creation access to Himself. It is not a relationship between equals but rather a relationship between deity and humanity. It is a father/child relationship, a teacher/student relationship, a king/subject, Lord/servant, Master/bond-slave, and savior/sinner relationship. It is a strong one/weak one relationship, an independent one and a totally dependent one relationship.

Since our relationships with God are so dependent upon Him, we rightly think of ourselves as looking up to Him. Our relationships with God, then, flow in a vertical direction.

The second type of relationship man was created to function in is sociological—relationships with other people. People relationships can be familial or non-familial. Unlike our relationship with God, these are relationships among equals, so they flow horizontally.

---

[34] https://www.phrases.org.uk/meanings/no-man-is-an-island.html, retrieved June 14, 2019

Two Levels of Relationships Chart #1

Direction (of Our Relationships)	**Vertical** (Relationship Between God and Man)	**Horizontal** (Relationships With Other People)

Table XIV

We express love to God with our worship. We express love to our fellow man with actions and words of respect. These relationships with God and with each other were never meant to be exclusive.

> *We love Him because He first loved us. If someone says, "I love God," and hates his brother, he is a liar; for he who does not love his brother whom he has seen, how can he love God whom he has not seen? And this commandment we have from Him: that he who loves God* **must** *love his brother also.*
> *1 John 4:19-21 (NKJV) emphasis added*

Our world is full of Christians who never get together with other believers to worship. A popular philosophy among them is, "Lord, I love you, but I can't stand Your people!" May I suggest that this position is exactly what Satan wants us to adopt.

To fulfill our purpose on earth requires that we live in a love relationship with God and with our fellow man. Without both relationships, humankind falls short of our divine purpose for existence.

HUMAN RELATIONSHIPS REQUIRE A CHAIN OF COMMAND

We worship God because of who He is and what He does. He is the Most High,[35] the Beginning and the End[36]. He deserves our love because He made us; we didn't make ourselves.[37] Satan destroyed the love relationship between him and God by trying to make it a relationship between equals, by trying to usurp God's position. Our love relationship

---

[35] Psalm 47:2
[36] Revelation 22:13
[37] Psalm 100:3

with God only works when we realize we are not God's equal and never will be.

Human relationships are between equals. No one should consider themselves better than anyone else; actually, we should think the opposite.

> *Let nothing be done through strife or vainglory; but in lowliness of mind let each esteem other better than themselves. Philippians 2:3 (KJV)*

> *For I say, through the grace given unto me, to every man that is among you, not to think of himself more highly than he ought to think; but to think soberly, according as God hath dealt to every man the measure of faith. Romans 12:3 (KJV)*

Humanity has always gotten into trouble when some people have thought about themselves as more equal than others by trying to elevate themselves in their own eyes or in the eyes of others.

> *For we dare not class ourselves or compare ourselves with those who commend themselves. But they, measuring themselves by themselves, and comparing themselves among themselves, are not wise. 2 Corinthians 10:12 (NKJV)*

> *Then Peter opened his mouth, and said, Of a truth I perceive that God is no respecter of persons: But in every nation he that feareth Him, and worketh righteousness, is accepted with Him. Acts 10:34-35 (KJV)*

> *Be of the same mind toward one another. Do not set your mind on high things, but associate with the humble. Do not be wise in your own opinion. Romans 12:16 (NKJV)*

In our human relationships it is necessary for some people to be in positions of authority over others. This does not mean that those in positions of authority are better and more deserving of that authority than those they are in authority over. God has made it clear to us that people in positions of authority are placed there by Him as representatives of His authority in those areas.

> *For the husband is the head of the wife, even as Christ is the head of the church: and He is the savior of the body. Therefore as the church is subject unto Christ, so let the wives be to their own husbands in everything. Ephesians 5:23-24 (KJV)*

> *Let every soul be subject to the governing authorities. For there is no authority except from God, and the authorities that exist are appointed by God. Therefore whoever resists the authority resists the ordinance of God, and those who resist will bring judgment on themselves. For rulers are not a terror to good works, but to evil. Do you want to be unafraid of the authority? Do what is good, and you will have praise from the same. For he is God's minister to you for good. But if you do evil, be afraid; for he does not bear the sword in vain; for he is God's minister, an avenger to execute wrath on him who practices evil. Therefore you must be subject, not only because of wrath but also for conscience' sake. For because of this you also pay taxes, for they are God's ministers attending continually to this very thing. Render therefore to all their due: taxes to whom taxes are due, customs to whom customs, fear to whom fear, honor to whom honor. Romans 13:1-7 (NKJV)*

> *Obey those who rule over you, and be submissive, for they watch out for your souls, as those who must give account. Let them do so with joy and not with grief, for that would be unprofitable for you. Hebrews 13:17 (NKJV)*

To those of us who are in positions of leadership and authority over our fellow man, we must not think that our authority is a symbol of greatness but rather as an opportunity for servanthood.

And whosoever of you will be the chiefest, shall be servant of all. Mark 10:44 (KJV)

Neither as being lords over God's heritage, but being examples to the flock. 1 Peter 5:3 (KJV)

In the kingdom of God, those who are in authority are not better than those they are leading. They are the ones chosen by God to be everyone's servant, to lead by example.

Two Levels of Relationships Chart #2

Relationships	**Vertical**	**Horizontal**
Positions	Not between equals	Between equals

Table XV

RELATIONSHIPS AND REDEMPTION

The message of redemption is fundamental to the Christian faith, but please permit me to address it in this context, even if it is a bit of a review for you. The first humans created by God sinned almost from the beginning. This sin separated all of mankind from the intended relationship with God. Sin also strained and destroyed the horizontal relationships between brothers, families, friends, and nations that God had intended for mankind.

Because sin destroyed all these relationships, God's plan from the beginning has always been reconciliation. Therefore, God implemented a redemption plan whereby He would redeem mankind back to Himself and back into harmony with each other.

*In Him we have **redemption through His blood**, the forgiveness of sins, according to the riches of His grace which He made to abound toward us in all wisdom and prudence, having made known to us the mystery of His will, according to His good pleasure which He purposed in Himself, that in the dispensation of the fullness of the times He might **gather together in one** all things in Christ, both which are in*

heaven and which are on earth—in Him. Ephesians 1:7-10
(NKJV) emphasis added

Notice that both levels of relationships are mentioned here in this scriptural description of God's redemption plan. We are redeemed back to God through Jesus' blood so that we will once again be joined together with our fellow man in unity of relationships.

Without being reconciled to God through Jesus, there is no hope of lasting, quality people relationships. But the healing and repairing of people relationships was part of what Jesus purchased for us on the cross with His blood.

Two Levels of Relationships Chart #3

Relationships	**Vertical**	**Horizontal**
Redemption *Ephesians 1:7-10*	*redemption through His blood*	*together in one*

Table XVI

RELATIONSHIPS AND COVENANT

The study of blood covenants is well worth your time. Covenants were in practice as far back as human history was recorded. They predate Abraham and were a way of life, and they were understood by everyone by the time Abraham was alive.

Blood covenants were not a religious practice, but they were the way agreements and commitments were made throughout every society. There were several silent rules, of which scholars say the ones listed below are the most important:

1. A blood covenant can never be broken once it is made.
2. If one party fails to keep their covenant, the other party in the covenant is obligated and expected to kill the one who broke covenant.
3. A blood covenant could be between two people, two families, or two nations.
4. A blood covenant applies to all future generations of those making the covenant. It never ends.

5. Everyone involved in a covenant are expected to honor it and defend it to the death, if need be. Honoring a covenant is not an option. You do it or you must die.

This is the way nations and families survived in prehistory and early history. If a group of people were attacked by an enemy more powerful than them, they would get word to those they were in covenant with, who would come and fight on their behalf. This way the family or nation ensured they would not be taken over by a hostile group or nation and would preserve their way of life for generations to come.

A covenant between two people was the forerunner of our marriage ceremony. Marriage is to be a commitment for life, which also affected all future generations. I'm glad we dropped the rule about killing the one who breaks the covenant though. The wedding ring worn on the fourth finger of the left hand replaced the cutting of hands to blend the blood from each person together as a public sign of the covenant the two people were making to each other.

Covenants between families or nations could also be made by a representative from each group mingling their blood together by cutting themselves. However, by the time God and Abraham made their covenant, it was common practice to kill an animal, split it into two halves, and have the two representatives walk between the two halves until their feet and sandals were soaked by the blood of that animal.

When you begin to understand blood covenants, Jesus' cross takes on a deeper meaning. The cross was the new covenant made between God and man, one where Jesus was chosen to be sacrificed. We cannot be partakers in this new covenant without being soaked in Jesus' blood. In other words, we only enter into this new covenant with God through declaring that Jesus, God's sacrificial lamb, is Lord.

God's redemption plan took many generations to unfold. Part of His plan included the Abrahamic covenant, out of which God established and chose a nation as His people, to exemplify the importance of both vertical relationships with Him and horizontal relationships with other people. God's people—the nation of Israel—were expected to obey His instructions regarding their relationship with Him and all their people relationships.

And God said unto Abraham, Thou shalt keep my **covenant** *therefore, thou, and thy seed after thee in their generations. Genesis 17:9 (KJV) emphasis added*

All covenants made between God and man have been made at a national or family level.[38] Therefore, we are all required to function as part of a nation or family for us to experience the benefits of the covenants with God. In other words, there are no "lone rangers" in the Kingdom of God. "No man is an island" in God's kingdom.

Two Levels of Relationships Chart #4

Relationships	**Vertical**	**Horizontal**
Covenant *Genesis 17:9*	*keep My covenant* between God and Abraham	*and thy seed after thee in their generations* nation of Israel

Table XVII

RELATIONSHIPS AND THE TEN COMMANDMENTS

Commandments were issued by God through Moses to instruct God's people of the importance of our vertical and horizontal relationships. This is the scripture where God gave us the Ten Commandments.

*You shall have **no other gods** before Me. You shall not make for yourself a **carved image**, or any likeness of anything that is in heaven above, or that is in the earth beneath, or that is in the water under the earth; you shall **not bow down to them** nor serve them. For I, the LORD your God, am a jealous God, visiting the iniquity of the fathers on the children to the third and fourth generations of those who hate Me, but showing mercy to thousands, to those who love Me and keep My commandments. You shall **not take the name of the LORD your God in vain**, for the LORD will not hold him guiltless who takes His name in vain. Remember **the Sabbath day, to keep it holy**. Six days you shall labor*

---

[38] Genesis 17:4

*and do all your work, but the seventh day is the Sabbath of the LORD your God. In it you shall do no work: you, nor your son, nor your daughter, nor your male servant, nor your female servant, nor your cattle, nor your stranger who is within your gates. For in six days the LORD made the heavens and the earth, the sea, and all that is in them, and rested the seventh day. Therefore the LORD blessed the Sabbath day and hallowed it. **Honor your father and your mother**, that your days may be long upon the land which the LORD your God is giving you. **You shall not murder. You shall not commit adultery. You shall not steal. You shall not bear false witness** against your neighbor. **You shall not covet** your neighbor's house; you shall not covet your neighbor's wife, nor his male servant, nor his female servant, nor his ox, nor his donkey, nor anything that is your neighbor's. Exodus 20:3-17 (NKJV) emphasis added*

Here are these commandments in a list.

The Ten Commandments

1. You shall have no other gods before Me.
2. You shall not make for yourself a carved image. You shall not bow down to them nor serve them.
3. You shall not take the name of the Lord your God in vain.
4. Remember the Sabbath day, to keep it holy.
5. Honor your father and your mother.
6. You shall not murder.
7. You shall not commit adultery.
8. You shall not steal.
9. You shall not bear false witness.
10. You shall not covet.

Of these original ten commandments, we see the first four deal with our relationship with God, and the last six deal with our relationships with mankind. They represent our vertical and horizontal relationships with

God and man and are the ultimate of what makes a strong relationship with both.

Two Levels of Relationships Chart #5

Relationships	Vertical	Horizontal
Ten Commandments *Exodus 20:3–17*	Commandments one through four	Commandments five through ten

Table XVIII

RELATIONSHIPS AND THE GREATEST COMMANDMENTS

To obey the ten commandments from a sense of duty is impossible to maintain for life. A strong will can only take a person so far, and a sense of duty will eventually produce death in anyone who lives by it.

There is only one heart motivation which has been proven to outlast life itself, that is love! Because of this, God has made it clear that He wants all our relationships to be based on or motivated by love. This is revealed in what Jesus called the two greatest commandments—to love God and love our fellow man.

> *Then one of them, a lawyer, asked Him a question, testing Him, and saying, "Teacher, which is the great commandment in the law?" Jesus said to him," 'You shall love the Lord your God with all your heart, with all your soul, and with all your mind.' This is the first and great commandment. And the second is like it: 'You shall love your neighbor as yourself.' On these two commandments hang all the Law and the Prophets. Matthew 22:35-40 (NKJV)*

Jesus said that what God was trying to tell us through Moses in the Ten Commandments, as well as in the expanded Law of Moses, was to love God and love our fellow man.

The rest of the Bible after the writings of Moses is called the writings of the prophets. They too, Jesus said, could be condensed into these two greatest commandments—love God and love each other. Jesus was saying that the entire Old Testament can be summarized with what He was calling the two greatest commandments.

Two Levels of Relationships Chart #6

Relationships	Vertical	Horizontal
Greatest Commandments *Matthew 22:35–40*	*love the Lord your God with your entire being*	*love your neighbor as yourself*

Table XIX

THESE RELATIONSHIPS MUST BE SIMULTANEOUS

As I have said previously, you can't have one relationship without the other. I have been the Music Pastor for several large churches throughout my life. At one church I was one of seven pastors. Every Thursday morning, we would gather in the senior pastor's office for a staff meeting to report what was happening within our respective departments. At one of these meetings I heard a fellow pastor say, "You know, ministry would be great if it weren't for the people." In case you didn't get his joke, without people there is no ministry. Without people there is no one to minister to.

As hard as it is to maintain a quality relationship with God, it is ten times more difficult to build and maintain relationships with other people, which is why it is so easy for Satan to encourage Christians to withdraw from worshiping with each other. We have all known countless Christians who used to be faithful to their local church but slipped into the attitude written about in a song by country music artist Tom T. Hall and made famous by many of country music's greatest singers. Here's the chorus of that song.

Me and Jesus got our own thing goin'
Me and Jesus got it all worked out
Me and Jesus got our own thing goin'
We don't need anybody to tell us what it's all about[39]

---

[39] © 1972 Sony/ATV Music Publishing LLC

The last line of this chorus sums up the dangerous attitude that Satan has successfully sold to millions of Christians. Satan's motive for pushing this lie on us is to dilute the punishment he receives when we assemble and praise God together. The Bible makes it clear that we can't claim a vertical relationship with God if our horizontal relationships are not intact.

> *If someone says, "I love God," and hates his brother, he is a liar; for he who does not love his brother whom he has seen, how can he love God whom he has not seen? And this commandment we have from Him: that he who loves God* ***must*** *love his brother also. 1 John 4:20-21 (NKJV) emphasis added*

If we have a problem with someone else, God doesn't recognize the love we express toward Him in worship until we change our attitude—especially, until we forgive—toward our fellow man. God does not receive our worship of Him until we forgive, or deal with the person or persons we are having issues with.

It is not only when we are the one having the problem with another person that God does not receive our worship.

> *Therefore if thou bring thy gift to the altar, and there rememberest that thy brother hath ought against thee; Leave there thy gift before the altar, and go thy way; first be reconciled to thy brother, and then come and offer thy gift. Matthew 5:23-24 (KJV)*

The word *ought* in this passage is old King James English for our word *anything*. In this verse we learn that we don't have to be the one in the relationship angry at the other person to disqualify our worship of God. If we try to ignore the fact that our brother or sister is upset with us yet think that everything will be all right between us and God, we are wrong. In that case, God specifically has instructed us to "first be reconciled" before returning and offering our worship to Him.

So we see, whether we are the one upset with someone else or someone is upset with us, our love relationship with God is jeopardized until these issues are worked out.

If we want to worship God, we must keep our horizontal relationships free from issues. We must also gather often to worship the Lord. It is imperative that we meet together and worship God on a regular basis! Do not fall for the lie of the devil who says it is all right to watch church on television or do devotions at home. Such an attitude plays right into the devil's trap. You cannot be nearly as effective against your enemy by staying home from church. This is why we were given this warning in the book of Hebrews.

> *Not forsaking the assembling of ourselves together, as the manner of some is; but exhorting one another: and so much the more, as ye see the day approaching. Hebrews 10:25 (KJV)*

Two Levels of Relationships Chart #7

Relationships	**Vertical**	**Horizontal**
Inclusive Relationships 1 John 4:20–21	*who loves God*	*must love his brother*

Table XX

RELATIONSHIPS WITH GOD AND HIS NATION

The congregation of the nation Israel was also called the church of the Old Testament.

> *This is he, that was in the **church** in the wilderness with the angel which spake to him in the mount Sinai . . . Acts 7:38a (KJV) emphasis added*

We are told that everything in the Old Testament was "types and shadows" of God's true plan to come.

> *So let no one judge you in food or in drink, or regarding a festival or a new moon or Sabbaths, which are a **shadow***

of things to come, but the substance is of Christ. Colossians 2:16-17 (NKJV) emphasis added

*For if He were on earth, He would not be a priest, since there are priests who offer the gifts according to the law; who serve the **copy (type) and shadow** of the heavenly things, as Moses was divinely instructed when he was about to make the tabernacle. For He said, "See that you make all things according to the pattern shown you on the mountain." But now He (Jesus) has obtained a more excellent ministry, inasmuch as He is also Mediator of a better covenant, which was established on better promises. Hebrews 8:4-6 (NKJV) emphasis added*

So, we see that the Old Testament church was made up of the nation of Israel, whom God chose to be His people through Abraham. But the true church today is made up of people who have believed and received Jesus as their Savior and Lord.

But as many as received Him, to them gave He power to become the sons of God, even to them that believe on His name: John 1:12 (KJV)

Therefore, the shadow church in the Old Testament gave way to the true Church, also called the nation or city of God, which was established by Jesus through the New Covenant between God and His new holy nation.

*But you have come to Mount Zion and to the city of the living God, the heavenly Jerusalem, to an innumerable company of angels, to the general assembly and **church** of the firstborn who are registered in heaven, to God the Judge of all, to the spirits of just men made perfect, to Jesus the Mediator of the new covenant, and to the blood of sprinkling that speaks better things than that of Abel. Hebrews 12:22-24 (NKJV) emphasis added*

> *Therefore, to you who believe, He is precious; but to those who are disobedient, "The Stone which the builders rejected has become the Chief Cornerstone," and "A Stone of stumbling and a Rock of offense." They stumble, being disobedient to the word, to which they also were appointed. But you are a chosen generation, a royal priesthood, a holy nation, His own special people, that you may proclaim the praises of Him who called you out of darkness into His marvelous light; who once were not a people but are now the people of God, who had not obtained mercy but now have obtained mercy. 1 Peter 2:7-10 (NKJV)*

Being God's priests speaks of our relationship with God. Being God's nation speaks of the horizontal relationships with people.

Two Levels of Relationships Chart #8

Relationships	**Vertical**	**Horizontal**
Nation of priests 1 Peter 2:7-10	*a royal priesthood*	*a holy nation*

Table XXI

RELATIONSHIPS AND ADOPTION

What I am about to say is controversial to some Christians who believe that the Jewish race is the chosen people of God. In the following verses, Paul makes it very clear who the true Jews are.

> *For he is not a Jew who is one outwardly, nor is circumcision that which is outward in the flesh; but he is a Jew who is one inwardly; and circumcision is that of the heart, in the Spirit, not in the letter; whose praise is not from men but from God. —Romans 2:28-29 (NKJV)*

> *For we are the circumcision, who worship God in the Spirit, rejoice in Christ Jesus, and have no confidence in the flesh. —Philippians 3:3 (NKJV)*

The Jewish nation of the old covenant was the "shadow nation," but we New Testament Christians are the true people of God according to these scriptures.

No longer are annual animal sacrifices required to establish our relationship with God since Jesus, the Lamb of God, was the complete, once and for all, sacrifice for mankind's sins.

> *The next day John saw Jesus coming toward him, and said, "Behold! The Lamb of God Who takes away the sin of the world!" John 1:29 (NKJV)*

Therefore, if we accept this sacrifice for our sins—Jesus, the Lamb of God—we are restored into right relationship with God through Jesus Christ.

> *Blessed be the God and Father of our Lord Jesus Christ, Who has blessed us with every spiritual blessing in the heavenly places in Christ, just as He chose us in Him before the foundation of the world, that we should be holy and without blame before Him in love, having predestined us to adoption as sons by Jesus Christ to Himself, according to the good pleasure of His will, Ephesians 1:3-5 (NKJV)*

Two Levels of Relationships Chart #9

Relationships	**Vertical**	**Horizontal**
Adoption *Ephesians 1:3-5*	*holy and without blame before Him in love*	*to adoption as sons by Jesus (family)*

Table XXII

RELATIONSHIPS AND SACRIFICES

Before Christ, the relationship between God and man was continually made possible through man's obedience to offer regular animal blood sacrifices.

*For the law, having a shadow of the good things to come, and not the very image of the things, can never with these same **sacrifices**, which they offer continually year by year, make those who approach perfect. For then would they not have ceased to be offered? For the worshipers, once purified, would have had no more consciousness of sins. But in those sacrifices there is a reminder of sins every year. For it is not possible that the blood of bulls and goats could take away sins. Hebrews 10:1-4 (NKJV) emphasis added*

Relationships with God have always been associated with sacrifice. Strong people-relationships have also been achieved through personal sacrifice, motivated by a high regard for the other person and demonstrated by thinking of others first instead of ourselves.

But a certain Samaritan, as he journeyed, came where he was: and when he saw him, he had compassion on him, And went to him, and bound up his wounds, pouring in oil and wine, and set him on his own beast, and brought him to an inn, and took care of him. And on the morrow when he departed, he took out two pence, and gave them to the host, and said unto him, Take care of him; and whatsoever thou spendest more, when I come again, I will repay thee. Luke 10:33-35 (KJV)

In this story the Samaritan built two strong relationships in a short period of time by living unselfishly. The first relationship was with the injured man who ended up owing his life to the Samaritan. Because of the Samaritan's selfless attitude, it is safe to assume that he would not have abused the injured man's gratitude toward him, which is a recipe for longevity in relationships.

The second strong relationship was with the inn keeper. We can assume that the Samaritan checked back with the inn keeper at a later date to see if he spent more money on the injured man than the Samaritan first gave him. Even if the Samaritan and the inn keeper did not become close friends, a friendship based on respect would have developed.

So, we see that quality people relationships result when mutual sacrifice occurs between people who are more concerned about others than themselves.

Two Levels of Relationships Chart #10

Relationships	Vertical	Horizontal
Sacrifices	*in those sacrifices there is a reminder of sins every year* Hebrews 10:1-4	*he had compassion on him* Luke 10:33-35

Table XXIII

RELATIONSHIPS AND NEW TESTAMENT SACRIFICES

In this section I will be referring to principles that I established in *Portrait of a Worshiper*. The overall premises of that book that apply to this section are:

- ➤ God created mankind for the purpose of worshiping Him.
- ➤ The way God designed and created mankind makes it possible for us to fulfill that purpose.
- ➤ God created us in three parts: spirit, soul and body.
- ➤ The body was given to mankind to express love to God and to each other.

Our vertical and horizontal relationships are established, maintained, and grown through sacrifices. But our sacrifices today are part of the new covenant, not the old one. Our sacrifices do not involve the shedding of blood since Jesus already shed His blood once and for all.[40] But we are still commanded to obey the sacrifices of the new covenant. To be partakers of the new covenant we must keep its conditions.

There are four New Testament sacrifices commanded under the New Covenant established through Jesus' blood. Two of these four apply to our vertical relationship with God, and two apply to our horizontal

---

[40] Hebrews 10:10

relationships with our fellow man. As far as I know, these are the only four sacrifices mentioned in the New Testament.

The First Sacrifice is found in Hebrews chapter 13, verse fifteen:

> *Therefore by Him let us continually offer the **sacrifice of praise** to God, that is, the fruit of our **lips**, giving thanks to His name. Hebrews 13:15 (NKJV) emphasis added*

The first sacrifice is the sacrifice of praise. Our praise and worship can be expressed in different ways with the various parts of our body. In this verse, the praise is being expressed with our lips.

To determine which expression of praise and worship this scripture in Hebrews is referring to as "the fruit of our lips," we must consider when is the first time we express praise with our lips. That would be the moment we declare Jesus is our Lord.

> *But what does it say? "The word is near you, in your mouth and in your heart" (that is, the word of faith which we preach): that if you **confess with your mouth the Lord Jesus** and believe in your heart that God has raised Him from the dead, you will be saved. For with the heart one believes unto righteousness, and **with the mouth confession is made** unto salvation. Romans 10:8-10 (NKJV) emphasis added*

The first time we offer praise to God with our lips has nothing to do with the way we feel in our emotions, but it has everything to do with declaring intelligently that Jesus is our Lord. Every person who comes to Christ MUST come this way, by confessing that Jesus is their Lord, which is the first expression of praise to Him, the fruit of our lips.

The Second Sacrifice is a progression from simply using our lips to express love to God to us getting to the place where we can use our entire body to praise God. God wants us to progress in the expressions of our praise and worship to Him to the place where we can offer praise to God in any way He desires from us, using any member of, and even all of, our body.

> *Therefore, I urge you, brothers, in view of God's mercy, to offer your **bodies as living sacrifices**, holy and pleasing to God—this is your spiritual **act of worship**. Romans 12:1 (NIV) emphasis added*

As we mature and grow in the Lord, our flesh dies in the sense that we want to please God more and not please our flesh. This maturing process allows us to express praise and worship to God with increasingly more of our body until we are able to express love to Him with our whole body. Our New Testament sacrifices to God start with our lips, then they progress to the point where we are able to use our entire body to express our love to God.

The Third and Fourth Sacrifices are for our people relationships and are inclusive, not progressive, so they must be done at the same time to be effective. Therefore, they are listed in the same Scripture, joined by an "and."

> *But to do good and to communicate forget not: for with such sacrifices God is well pleased. Hebrews 13:16 (KJV)*

Again, these two New Testament sacrifices toward mankind are *inclusive.* Doing only one of these sacrifices can cause disaster because one is not complete without the other.

If we are always doing good for the people in our lives, for example, but we never communicate with them, our relationships will become shallow. Marital relationships, which are expected to be physically intimate, will eventually disintegrate if there is no emotional intimacy and if it's not fueled by communication. Workaholic fathers may shower their children with lavish gifts, but after a while their children only desire time with them, which must be invested in to facilitate communication.

On the other hand, I have known many people who are quick to communicate but never consider the effects their words will have on the ones they are communicating with. Many of these people are proud to be someone who "shoots from the hip" or one who will "tell it like it is." If we always communicate with no thought of doing good through our speech, we will injure and devastate the people in our lives. If you are one who tells it like it is or speaks before thinking, then consider this verse.

> *Let no corrupt communication proceed out of your mouth, but that which is good to the use of edifying, that it may minister grace unto the hearers. Ephesians 4:29 (KJV)*

For human relationships to flourish, these sacrifices must be in operation at the same time.

Two Levels of Relationships Chart #11

Relationships	Vertical	Horizontal
New Testament Sacrifices	Progressive Sacrifice **#1** *the fruit of our* **lips** *Hebrews 13:15* Sacrifice **#2** *your* **bodies** *Romans 12:1*	Inclusive Sacrifice **#3** *to do good* Sacrifice **#4** *and to communicate* *Hebrews 13:16*

Table XXIV

SUMMARY

Notice that to do the four New Testament sacrifices is to obey the two greatest commandments of God. In turn, this will help us to obey all the original Ten Commandments, which means we will obey what the Bible tells us we must do to have a love relationship with God and our fellow man. The reason we need strong relationships in both directions is so we can function as worshipers of God as part of a group.

On the following page is the complete Two Levels of Relationships chart that you can study in one glance.

Complete Two Levels of Relationships Chart

Direction of Relationships	Vertical Relationship between God and man	Horizontal Relationships with each other
Positions	Not between equals	Between equals
Redemption Ephesians 1:7-10	*redemption through His blood*	*together in one*
Covenant Genesis 17:9	*keep My covenant* between God and Abraham	*and thy seed after thee in their generations* nation of Israel
Ten Commandments Exodus 20:3-17	Commandments one through four	Commandments five through ten
Greatest Commandments Matthew 22:35-40	*love the Lord your God with your entire being*	*love your neighbor as yourself*
Inclusive Relationships 1 John 4:20-21	*who loves God*	*must love his brother*
Nation of priests 1 Peter 2:7-10	*a royal priesthood*	*a holy nation*
Adoption Ephesians 1:3-5	*holy and without blame before Him in love*	*to adoption as sons by Jesus (family)*
Sacrifices	*in those sacrifices there is a reminder of sins every year* Hebrews 10:1-4	*he had compassion on him* Luke 10:33-35
New Testament Sacrifices	Progressive Sacrifice **#1** *the fruit of our **lips*** Hebrews 13:15 Sacrifice **#2** *your **bodies*** Romans 12:1	Inclusive Sacrifice **#3** *to do good* Sacrifice **#4** *and to communicate* Hebrews 13:16

Table XXV

CHAPTER FIVE

"THE DEVICE OF UNFORGIVENESS"

KNOWING THE ENEMY

So, here's the situation. We were created to worship God as a means of punishing the devil. We were promised great effectiveness against the devil when we worship God in unity with other believers. Our enemy knows this, and he will never stop trying to destroy all human relationships we have so that our worship of God will be weak and ineffective against him.

In international warfare, billions of dollars are spent on gathering intelligence about the enemy because the more you know about your enemy, the more likely you are to get the upper hand in the war.

In spiritual warfare it is also very important to know how the enemy fights so we are the ones with the advantage.

> *Lest Satan should get an advantage of us: for we are not*
> *ignorant of his devices. 2 Corinthians 2:11 (KJV)*

This statement is very important for us to understand as Christians charged with executing the judgements of God upon Lucifer and his followers. Remember, if we do not praise God with high praises, Lucifer is not punished. What's more, he's allowed to attack us in the two parts of our being that aren't yet redeemed: our souls and our bodies.

Either we will attack Lucifer with our high praises of God, or he will attack us with his devices. There is no such thing as a cease-fire agreement in spiritual warfare. Let's read this scripture again in a different translation to see if it gives you further clarity.

> *. . . in order that Satan might not outwit us. For we are not unaware of his schemes. 2 Corinthians 2:11 (NIV)*

The context of this scripture is very important because it reveals the major device Satan uses to attack human relationships. Here is the verse right before it.

> *To whom ye forgive anything, I forgive also: for if I forgave anything, to whom I forgave it, for your sakes forgave I it in the person of Christ; Lest Satan . . . 2 Corinthians 2:10-11a (KJV)*

There are many devices of the enemy, and Paul has instructed us to become aware of them all. Since I'm talking about guarding against satanic attacks on our relationships, I will focus on the device of the devil called unforgiveness.

THE IMPORTANCE OF FORGIVENESS

We live in a fallen world, and all of humanity are sinners in need of a Savior; therefore, we all make mistakes. Our mistakes affect us as well as everyone around us. When mistakes happen, someone will get hurt or offended.

> *Woe unto the world because of offences! for it must needs be that offences come; but woe to that man by whom the offence cometh! Matthew 18:7 (KJV)*

At this time, I would like to quote a verse from the long-lost book of Hezekiah[41]: *If a man take offense, give him the gate also.* OK, so maybe it wasn't that funny.

Because we are human, there will always be offenses. It is how we handle the offences that makes the difference for us.

There is a way to guard against being offended, which is found in this verse.

---

[41] This is not a true book of the Bible. This is meant to be a joke.

Great peace have they which love thy law: and nothing shall offend them. Psalm 119:165 (KJV)

The more we spend time in the word of God and the more we are taught by the Holy Spirit, the more we will be able to shake off the offenses of this life. Until that happens, God has given us a powerful tool so we can deal with all the offenses we encounter in our lives. It is called forgiveness. Without forgiveness we are doomed. There is no other way to protect ourselves against the cancer of bitterness.

*Pursue peace with all people, and holiness, without which no one will see the Lord: looking carefully lest anyone fall short of the grace of God; lest any **root of bitterness** springing up cause trouble, and by this many become defiled; Hebrews 12:14-15 (NKJV) emphasis added*

Bitterness is more contagious than a communicable disease. It will infect every person it touches if they have not been inoculated by the word of God. Jesus taught us about the importance of forgiving when He taught the disciples how to pray. Here is the model prayer Jesus taught in the Sermon on the Mount:

*After this manner therefore pray ye: Our Father which art in heaven, Hallowed be Thy name. Thy kingdom come, Thy will be done in earth, as it is in heaven. Give us this day our daily bread. And **forgive us** our debts, **as we forgive** our debtors. And lead us not into temptation, but deliver us from evil: For Thine is the kingdom, and the power, and the glory, forever. Amen. Matthew 6:9-13 (KJV) emphasis added*

After Jesus recited this prayer for us to learn as a model for our prayers, He continued teaching. I have heard multiple sermon series on the Lord's prayer lasting weeks to several months. However, when Jesus taught about this prayer, He only chose one topic out of this entire model prayer to teach about. That should tell us how important this one topic is. The topic Jesus chose to comment on was forgiveness, and here's what He said.

> *For if ye **forgive men** their trespasses, your heavenly Father will also **forgive you**: But if ye **forgive not men** their trespasses, **neither** will your Father **forgive your trespasses**. Matthew 6:14-15 (KJV) emphasis added*

The prayer that Jesus taught demonstrates that He wants us to ask God to forgive us "as" (to the degree that) we forgive others. Just in case we did not catch that, Jesus underscored this point after the model prayer. He said it twice—once from a positive stance and once from a negative stance. After Jesus' comment, there should be no doubt in our minds that, if we don't forgive others, God will not forgive us.

Who among us has any chance of making it without God's forgiveness? None of us.

> *For all have sinned, and come short of the glory of God; Romans 3:23 (KJV)*

We all sin, make mistakes every day, and require the forgiveness of the Lord to escape eternal damnation. Without God's forgiveness we are doomed for eternity. But the only way we can get God's forgiveness is to forgive others ourselves.

THE UNFORGIVING SERVANT

The Lord's prayer is not the only time Jesus taught about forgiveness. Here is a parable He told that gives further insight on this topic.

> *²³ Therefore is the kingdom of heaven likened unto a certain king, which would take account of his servants.*
>
> *²⁴ And when he had begun to reckon, one was brought unto him, which owed him ten thousand talents.*
>
> *²⁵ But forasmuch as he had not to pay, his lord commanded him to be sold, and his wife, and children, and all that he had, and payment to be made.*
>
> *²⁶ The servant therefore fell down, and worshiped him, saying, Lord, have patience with me, and I will pay thee all.*

²⁷ Then the lord of that servant was moved with compassion, and loosed him, and forgave him the debt.

²⁸ But the same servant went out, and found one of his fellow servants, which owed him an hundred pence: and he laid hands on him, and took him by the throat, saying, Pay me that thou owest.

²⁹ And his fellow servant fell down at his feet, and besought him, saying, Have patience with me, and I will pay thee all.

³⁰ And he would not: but went and cast him into prison, till he should pay the debt.

³¹ So when his fellow servants saw what was done, they were very sorry, and came and told unto their lord all that was done.

³² Then his lord, after that he had called him, said unto him, O thou wicked servant, I forgave thee all that debt, because thou desiredst me:

³³ Shouldest not thou also have had compassion on thy fellow servant, even as I had pity on thee?

³⁴ And his lord was wroth, and delivered him to the tormentors, till he should pay all that was due unto him.

³⁵ So likewise shall my heavenly Father do also unto you, if ye from your hearts forgive not every one his brother their trespasses. Matthew 18:23-35 (KJV)

It is obvious that the way debt was handled then is not the way debt is handled today—and thank God for that. This was also a time when slavery was the norm. In this story, the lord who owned the slave who owed him money reasoned that selling the slave, his wife, and his kids was the best way he would recoup some of his money. I can hear him say to himself and his slave, "It's not personal, it's just business."

No wonder why the slave fell at the lord's feet and begged for another chance. To the master it was all about settling an old debt, but to the servant it was about keeping his family together. If the plans had gone through, the servant would have never seen his family again.

How much would you worship and beg if someone was about to split up your family? The servant must have made quite the impassioned plea because the lord didn't just give him another chance to pay the debt, he forgave the entire debt, thereby giving this servant the assurance that his family would never be torn apart at any time in the future. What a wonderful gift. The verse states that the lord was moved with compassion. For most hard-nosed businessmen that I know, it takes quite a bit to move them to compassion, so this must have been quite the performance by the servant.

Verse twenty-seven tells us the lord did two things after the servant made his appeal. The first thing he did was loosed the servant. When we choose not to forgive someone, that is our attempt to bind them or hold them hostage. Part of forgiving someone is to release them from all expectations and debt. Of course, the second thing he did was to forgive the entire debt. Forgiveness is an all-or-nothing deal. It is not forgiveness if it is only partial. It does not work to say, "I'll forgive you for this but not for that."

Almost all theologians agree that the lord in this story represents God, and the servants represent God's people. They also believe that the enormous debt owed is the price of our salvation. God had to come down from heaven in the form of Jesus and pay our debt for our sin. With that debt paid, we can now be forgiven for all our sins and become part of God's family.

The trouble comes when we, like the servant in the story, forget how much we have been forgiven and treat our fellow servants the way this servant did. I don't care what anybody does to us to offend us—it will never come close to the level of offence our sin has brought to God. The moral of the story is that if God has forgiven us so much, then we ought to forgive our fellow servants whenever we are offended by them.

In our story, the servant who did not forgive his fellow servant was "delivered to the tormentors" until the debt was dealt with. The second part of this is found in verse thirty-five, which says:

> So likewise shall my heavenly Father do also unto you,
> if ye from your hearts forgive not every one his brother their
> trespasses. Matthew 18:35 (KJV)

If we do not forgive someone for an offense, we are the one who will be tormented until we forgive them. In this verse there seems to be a difference between being put in debtors' prison to pay off a debt and being delivered to the tormentors. It is true that if you have offended someone you can feel as if you are in bondage to them; however, that does not compare with the torment someone goes through when they have not forgiven someone.

CHAPTER SIX

"PROTECTING OUR RELATIONSHIPS"

The Importance of Humility

One of the most important things we do in our lives is protect and maintain our relationships. This starts with our relationship with God, Who is the object of our worship. It also includes our horizontal relationships, which makes our worship powerful against the enemy.

To protect our relationship with God, we must be quick to repent and own our mistakes. In the 1970s I heard this saying for the first time:

> ## If you feel far from GOD, guess who moved!

If there is a problem with our relationship with God, the problem is not on His end. He is perfect in all His ways. We, on the other hand, are prone to selfishness, self-centeredness, and self-exaltation. These qualities biblically qualify us to be resisted by God.

Likewise, you younger people, submit yourselves to your elders. Yes, all of you be submissive to one another, and be clothed with humility, for
"God resists the proud,
But gives grace to the humble." 1 Peter 5:5 (NKJV)

Humility is also of paramount importance when it comes to our horizontal relationships as well.

I am in my seventies and have walked with God since my early twenties. Throughout the course of my life I have been tremendously affected by thousands of sermons. If, however, you asked me to rehearse any of them, I would only remember bits and pieces of the sermons I could count on one hand.

There is, however, one sermon I heard in the 1970s that I remember to this day. Peter Marshall Junior spoke a simple exegesis of these verses.

But if we walk in the light, as He is in the light, we have fellowship one with another, and the blood of Jesus Christ His Son cleanseth us from all sin. If we say that we have no sin, we deceive ourselves, and the truth is not in us. 1 John 1:7-8 (KJV)

The Friendly People had been asked to do music for Peter Marshall Junior's camp meeting in upstate New York. More than 2,000 people crowded inside the tent where the meeting was held, and at least three to four hundred people were outside the tent the night we were there.

The Friendly People had done mainly upbeat songs that evening, and the crowd was electric with energy and joy when we turned the stage over to the speaker. Peter Marshall Jr.'s seriousness and stoic face was in complete contrast to the mood of the evening so far, but soon his seriousness dictated the emotional tenor of everyone there. He spoke for an hour and a half.

The Holy Spirit taught me through that sermon that night. While this is not necessarily the way he presented his thoughts, this is my understanding of his message.

1. There is a subtle difference between God being light and God being "in" the light.

In chapter 1 of First John, light is attributed to God in two ways. Here is the first way:

> *This then is the message which we have heard of Him, and declare unto you, that God is light, and in Him is no darkness at all. 1 John 1:5 (KJV)*

The light of God is actual light, which is the opposite of darkness. We see that in how John described the new heaven (also known as "the new Jerusalem").

> *And the city had no need of the sun, neither of the moon, to shine in it: for the glory of God did lighten it, and the Lamb is the light thereof. Revelation 21:23 (KJV)*

The glory of God is revealed in our natural world as physical light. That glory is what Isaiah was referring to in chapter sixty.

> *Arise, shine; For your light has come! And the glory of the Lord is risen upon you. Isaiah 60:1 (NKJV)*

Please notice that the glory of the Lord, His light, must rise upon us so we can shine, and we must first get into position to receive that light by arising. The glory of God that is revealed on us is indeed His glory, not ours.

The second way John speaks of light and God is found two verses later in First John. In that scripture John uses the phrase "He is in the light." The light in verse five refers to God's glory. The light in 1 John 1:7 refers to God's truth. We even say when someone discovers truth that they have become "enlightened." "They are walking in new light." Jesus, who is God, declared He is the "Truth."

*Jesus saith unto him, I am the way, **the truth**, and the life: no man cometh unto the Father, but by Me. John 14:6 (KJV) emphasis added*

God is light because God is truth. Truth brings glory, and glory is manifested within our physical realm as light. We cannot be our own light because we are not truth. God is the source of enlightenment because God is the source of **all** truth. If we desire to walk in God's glory, we must walk in truth.

Therefore, the promise found in verse seven could read like this: "If we walk in the truth as God is Truth, as God is the source of all truth, as God is **in** all truth, then we have fellowship with each other." When we discover truth of any kind, we discover God in that truth because God is the source of it.

2. There is a particular truth that will allow us to have fellowship with each other. Everyone who walks in this truth is guaranteed to be positioned to have fellowship with his fellow man, and those who don't walk in this truth will not.

If we say that we have no sin, we deceive ourselves, and the truth is not in us. 1 John 1:8 (KJV)

Whenever we get to the place that we feel we cannot be wrong (which is another way of saying we cannot sin), we have deceived ourselves. As a matter of fact, that attitude guarantees that we cannot learn what is truth in that situation. It also guarantees to destroy our horizontal relationships and prevent us from having fellowship with others.Peter Marshall, Jr. explored this in depth during his sermon, and as he did, I experienced many strong emotions and extreme thought processes. He said things like this:

➢ If I think I understand all of the truth about a subject, I am deceived.
➢ If I think I cannot be wrong, I am deceived.
➢ If I think I will never do anything wrong in any given circumstance, I am deceived.

> ➤ If I think I do not have the capability of stealing, I am deceived.
> ➤ If I think I do not have the capability of coveting, I am deceived.
> ➤ If I think I do not have the capability of murdering someone, I am deceived.
> ➤ I am no different than any person who is incarcerated for a crime, and I have the same capability and sin nature that they have. But for the grace of God, there go I!

The point is that if we think of ourselves with humility, we are positioned to have strong relationships with other people. Without humility, we will sabotage our relationships with people and with God.

TRUTH

Truth is absolute. There is only one truth about every subject, natural or spiritual. All truths have their origin in God.

Since the 1980s, school systems have been teaching relative truths. Relative truth means that truth to one person may not be truth to another and that everyone has the right to believe in their own truth. This is absolutely not the Bible teaching about truth. Just because I believe something is true does not make it true.

My wife's mother is ninety-four years old. She has been an independent woman since 1974 when Chris' father passed away from complications of multiple sclerosis. Her mother has a relatively sharp mind and passes the mental cognitive tests that the state requires to determine if she can make her own decisions.

In her mind she is still the independent person of twenty to thirty years ago; yet in reality, her severe arthritis and osteoporosis has made it difficult for her to move around, and the lack of movement has caused her muscles to weaken to the place where she cannot take care of herself anymore. Last week we spent an entire night in the emergency room with her because she thought she could stand on her own but fell and hit her head when she tried. Yet still, in her mind, she thinks she can live alone. That is her truth; but in reality, it is a lie.

I understand why Chris' mother thinks she can still take care of herself because I face the same situation every day. In my mind I am a virile man in my forties. The problem is, when I look in the mirror, I ask myself,

"Who is that old man?" I believe I can still do everything I did thirty years ago—until I try to do it. Then I am faced with the reality the truth, that my body does not function like it did back then.

These are examples of how our personal truths are not true and how dangerous it can be to believe something is true when it is not. The most important thing we can do when learning is to find out the truth from God's perspective, not what we or someone else thinks is the truth.

This approach requires that we consider every subject with the attitude that neither we nor any others have a handle on the truth. Only God knows the whole truth. We should never trust anything we believe is true, and we should never trust anything anyone has taught us is truth. Compared with the actual truth, Paul tells us we should consider ourselves as liars.

> For what if some did not believe? Will their unbelief make the faithfulness of God without effect? Certainly not! Indeed, let **God** be **true** but every **man** a **liar**. As it is written:
> "That you may be justified in your words,
> And may overcome when you are judged." Romans 3:3-4 (NKJV) emphasis added

Even if we do not believe the truth, that does not change the fact that it is truth. Compared with our knowledge of truth against God's knowledge of truth, we are all liars. We know very little of the truth compared to God. Even if we have spent our entire lives studying a subject, we will never know enough about it to be considered anything more than a liar compared to God's knowledge of that subject. If we adopt any other attitude but this one, it will guarantee that we will not be able to fellowship with someone who believes differently from us, which will weaken our group worship.

It is interesting to me that, according to the Scripture, there are two things that will take place when we adopt this attitude that, compared to God, we are all liars. The first thing is *that you may be justified in your words.* If you are a person who always has to be right, you will alienate others from yourself. But, if you adopt the attitude that you could be wrong, you will attract others to yourself, making it possible for others to validate or justify your words. To justify what someone says is to understand why they say it, not to validate it as truth.

The second result from adopting this attitude is that you *"may overcome when you are judged."* If you are convinced you are right and someone judges you as being wrong, it can be devastating in one of two ways. Our tendency when judged by other people is to either be hurt by their judgment or to entrench ourselves further into what we believe even if we have no evidence which supports that position. If, however, you adopt the attitude that you could be wrong, it will be not be a shock to your system when someone tells you that you're wrong. Following this approach will ensure that we will overcome when we are judged because we won't be devastated.

BEING AGREED

In the Old Testament book of Amos, we read this question.

> *Can two walk together, except they be agreed? Amos 3:3 (KJV)*

At first, we may think this question is rhetorical. It seems reasonable that two people cannot walk together and accomplish a common goal unless they agree with each other. However, I would like to suggest that the answer to this question is yes.

How can two people walk together yet not be in agreement? The answer to this question is found in what we have been discussing in this book. The first condition that must be present for people who do not agree to do anything together is they must consider themselves capable of being wrong or being able to sin. The second condition is for everyone in a relationship should walk in forgiveness toward each other.

In chapter 1 we read the verses that said we need to speak the same thing and be of the same mind. I explained how music allows us to speak the same thing at the same time with the same meaning and emotions. Now let me address what it means to be of the same mind.

Being of the same mind does not mean being in agreement with someone. It means having the same attitude of humility that we all are considered liars in comparison to what God says is truth. That is the mind that we need to have in order to worship together and cause damage to the kingdom of darkness with our worship of Almighty God.

> *Let this mind be in you, which was also in Christ Jesus: Who, being in the form of God, thought it not robbery to be equal with God: But made Himself of no reputation, and took upon Him the form of a servant, and was made in the likeness of men: And being found in fashion as a man, He humbled Himself, and became obedient unto death, even the death of the cross. Philippians 2:5-8 (KJV)*

Jesus does not take anything away from God the father by being Emanuel (God with us). But it is the attitude that Jesus adopted when He came to earth that He wants us to adopt.

➢ He made Himself of no reputation.
➢ He took the form of a servant.
➢ He was made in the likeness of man.
➢ He humbled Himself.
➢ He became obedient.
➢ He laid down His life for others.
➢ He died in the cruelest way known to mankind.

In short, Jesus' mind or attitude was humility, which is what God expects from us so that our relationships will be well maintained and our group worship will be extremely effective.

Christians grow by receiving revelation knowledge from the word of God and the Holy Spirit. No one grows spiritually without having their mind renewed or changed. Therefore, what we believed to be true last year may not be what we believe is true this year. This growing dynamic means God does not expect us to always agree with each other. He only expects us to walk in humility toward each other so we do not bite and devour one another[42] in our pursuit of truth.

Our time on earth is designated as the time for us to work out our

---

[42] Galatians 5:15

own salvation[43] by having our minds renewed.[44] Each of us will learn and grow at different paces, so there will be times when we don't agree with each other. Those are not the times to separate from each other, but those are the times to walk in humility and forgiveness.

As long as we are on this earth, we will only know small parts of the truth.[45] However, when we graduate from this life, we will know everything God knows.

> *For now we see through a glass, darkly; but then face to face: now I know in part; but then shall I know even as also I am known. 1 Corinthians 13:12 (KJV)*

So, I will know truth in heaven the way God knows me now. How well does God know me? God knows the thoughts and intents of my heart.[46] God knows the end from the beginning.[47] God predestined my destiny.[48] God knows the number of hairs I have left on my head.[49] God knows everything about me, so one day I will know everything as well. But until that day, the amount of truth I know only qualifies me to be a liar. But the longer I walk with God, the more I am putting on the mind of Christ.[50] Remember, the mind of Christ is humility and forgiveness, not knowledge. Complete knowledge only comes when we leave this earth.

GOD INTENDS FOR US TO SEARCH FOR TRUTH

Only God knows all truth. Knowing that while on earth humans would be expected to search for the truth, God gave mankind a unique cognitive ability called deductive reasoning—the ability to fill in the blanks with theories and guesses so we can come up with an overall

---

[43] Philippians 2:12
[44] Romans 12:2
[45] 1 Corinthians 13:9
[46] Hebrews 4:12
[47] Revelations 22:13
[48] Ephesians 1:5
[49] Matthew 10:30
[50] 1 Corinthians 2:16

understanding of a concept of truth. We may never get all the details right, but at least we can come up with the overall idea.

Some of mankind's theories are nonsensical, which is why we need to be led by the Holy Spirit as we are seeking truth. We also need to hold up our understandings against the Word of Truth to ensure what we believe is confirmed by the Bible.

Truth will not just plop into our laps. God intends for us to search out truths, and for truth to come at a great price to us.

> *It is the glory of God to conceal a matter, But the glory of kings is to search out a matter. Proverbs 25:2 (NKJV)*

> *But we speak the wisdom of God in a mystery, the hidden wisdom which God ordained before the ages for our glory, 1 Corinthians 2:7 (NKJV)*

TRUTH IS A GIFT FROM GOD

Since God is the source of all truth, mathematical truth, scientific truth, as well as spiritual truth; He must impart to us the ability to receive and understand it. If we are not humble, if we are not quick to repent, and if we do not maintain the attitude that we can be wrong, there is no way God can impart truth to us.

We have already read this verse, but I would like to read it again in light of these statements.

> *In meekness instructing those that oppose themselves; if God peradventure will give them repentance to the acknowledging of the truth; 2 Timothy 2:25 (KJV)*

Again, God gives grace to the humble, and to the humble He reveals truth. Without God we cannot understand truth of any kind. If we are humble, God reveals truth to us. If we are not humble, we are already deceived.

CHAPTER SEVEN

"PEOPLE RELATIONSHIP FILES"

Gaining Understanding

In this last chapter I would like to offer some further insights as to how to protect and maintain our people relationships so our worship together will be as effective as it can be. This chapter should be considered as a continuation of the study of anthropology found in *Portrait of a Worshiper*. The reason I did not include this chapter in that book is because I needed to make the case for why it is important to worship with other Christians.

In *Portrait of a Worshiper* I established the biblical understanding that humans are comprised of their spirit, soul, and body.[51] I also established that a human soul is comprised of mind, will, and emotions.[52]

In the ninth chapter of that book I explained how we gain natural understanding. We come to natural understanding when we process the data received from our five senses with the three parts of our soul.

Our brain is like a computer that is programmed to create files for every event or experience we have in our lives. We also create files for every relationship we have or every person we know about.

While we are going through an experience, our brain will keep every detail about it in our file because it is impossible to fully process an experience while it's happening, including which data is important to keep or which data to discard. Every experience we go through requires continual analyzation of the data because all experiences in life are interactive. We

---

[51] 1 Thessalonians 5:23
[52] Nee, *Spiritual Man*

must continually analyze the data we are receiving in order to plot our next moves or words.

The natural data we receive in every experience comes from our five senses—seeing, hearing, touching, tasting, and smelling. Therefore, the questions we are always on alert to answer are:

1. What are we seeing in this experience?
2. What are we hearing in this experience?
3. What are we physically feeling in this experience?
4. What are the tastes of this experience?
5. What are the smells of this experience?

Every time we enter data from the five senses into a current event file in our mind, we piece more of the puzzle of that event together using that data to help us reach the answers to these questions:

1. What conclusions can we derive from this event or entry? OR **What do we think** about this event or entry?
2. What do our emotions register from this event or entry? OR **What do we feel** (emotionally) about this event or entry?
3. What is the best course of action, if any, that we should take because of this event or entry? OR **What will we do** about this event or entry?

The answers to these three questions make up our understanding of and our interaction with that current event. Here is a fictitious event file. Study this to understand the way we process every event file in our lives.

Example Event File #1

New Event Title or Identifying Mental Image: *Pending*
Other Pertinent Information:

Time	Sense	Data	Mind	Emotions	Will
noon	Hear	Boom or crash outside the house	What was that?	Startled, curious	Find out what it was

	See	See nothing out the window	What could that have been?	Curious, concerned, anxious	Go outside to investigate
12:01 pm	Smell	Smell something burning when door opens	What type of fire is that smell? It is not wood or BBQ.	Concerned, anxious, nervous	Continue to investigate
	See	See flames and black smoke on street corner	Something's on fire! What is it?	Fear	Run to see what it is
12:02 pm	Touch	Feel heat from flame 10 feet away	I'd better stay back.	Fear	Call for help

Table XXVI

After the event is over, the file is usually reviewed, at least briefly. Sometimes this happens in our sleep. At that time we may name the event for a future quick reference like "Street Corner Fire;" most likely we'll just identify the file with a mental image of the event.

During that review of the file, we'll determine if any irrelevant data entries can be discarded. We will also record our final conclusions concerning this event and place them first in the file so that when we search through our memory files at a later time, all we need to review for each file is the summary page that contains these three processed conclusions:

1. What did we think about this event?
2. What did we emotionally feel about this event?
3. What did we do about this event?

WHY?

If other people are involved in an event, there is one more question that will arise regarding every entry we make in our event files involving a person. This simply speaks to the reason someone does what they do or says what they say. The answer to the question "why" on an entry can drastically change what goes in the last three columns of our event file.

When people are involved in a life event, our event file looks like this:

Example Event File #2

New Event Title or Identifying Mental Image:

Other Pertinent Information:

Time	Sense	Data	Who	Why	Mind	Emotions	Will

Table XXVII

In addition to event files, our brains also create files for every person we know or have heard of. The event files where these people are involved are linked to these people's files in that an entry in an event file of actions or words by a person will automatically be entered into that person's file as an observation.

The primary purpose of our people files is to help us answer why a person has done or said something. However, it can take a long time to get to know another individual's heart well enough to confidently know their motives. We should never arrive quickly or flippantly at the answer to why.

Please do not be quick to judge another person's motives. I personally believe it can be a deception from the enemy to believe you are a quick judge of character. First impressions can be deceiving and wrong. If you feel prompted to fill in the "why" column before you have invested the time to get to know a person, you should assume that the prompting is from the enemy. The exception to this rule is for those who operate the spiritual gift of discerning of spirits.

Healthy relationships are formed between people who are slow to answer why. God-ordained relationships can be cut short when we are quick to answer this question. Answering this question incorrectly is the most deadly and dangerous thing we can do when it comes to our relationships. There is nothing wrong with leaving the "why" column blank in our event files for months or years after we have first met someone.

People Files

Here's what our people files look like:

People Files #1

Visual Images of the Person:

Name and other pertinent information we learn as the relationship develops:

Event File Link	Observation	Questionable Action	Personal Timer	(Possible) Motivation(s)
			000.000	

Table XXVIII

As we go through life and encounter other people, we will populate their observations column with the things they do and say. A person who has not been hurt by others in the past will probably have a much longer list of observations before they come across an action or statement that is questionable.

Once an observation becomes questionable and we transfer it into the questionable actions column, an internal timer is started. When the timer runs out, we will have no choice but to fill in the motivation column. It does not matter who we are—when the timer runs out, we have to answer why, which means we have to put something in the motivation column. We will not be able to avoid it, even if it is only our best guess!

When the motivation column is filled in on that person's file, the why column on the event file is automatically filled in as well. That will set off a chain reaction in the files, and we will then have to reprocess them based on this new data. Observations that were not questionable before will suddenly become questionable to us as we search the observations list for validation of our motivation conclusion.

People who have been hurt in the past will have a shorter time set on their timer. With a little practice, you should be able to figure out where your internal timer is set so you have an idea of how much time you have to go through the process of determining the motivation of someone.

DETERMINING MOTIVATIONS OF OTHERS

Whether or not we realize it, we use one or more of these approaches when trying to determine someone's motives:

1. We ask the person directly why they did what they did.

This is the scariest approach to finding out the truth of someone's motives and is the approach we avoid the most. Interestingly, it is also the only biblical approach.

> *Moreover if your brother sins against you, go and tell him his fault between you and him alone. If he hears you, you have gained your brother. Matthew 18:15 (NKJV)*

Seldomly do we take the biblical approach of going to the other person and asking them about their motivation for doing something. People tend not to like taking this approach because:

  a. We do not want them to know we are questioning any of their actions.
  b. We are not sure how they will respond if we tell them we're questioning their actions.
  c. We do not want to jeopardize losing the relationship by being honest with them.
  d. We are not sure if the questionable action is serious enough for the risk or if we should wait for a more serious one before we confront them.

If we choose this approach of talking to the person about the questionable action, we must endeavor to do it without accusations (presupposing their motives) and with meekness and humility.

> *Brethren, if a man be overtaken in a fault, ye which are spiritual, restore such an one in the spirit of meekness; considering thyself, lest thou also be tempted. Galatians 6:1 (KJV)*

We must always approach our brother without passion or strong emotions. This is what it means to be careful not to be tempted to offend them when we are trying to help them and help ourselves.

2. We try to figure out on our own what their motivation was.

This is probably the most used method to determine the why of a questionable action by others. We usually make a list of the possible motivations that someone could have had when they acted questionably. These may range from the very cynical to the very innocent. Our list of possible motivations will be greatly influenced by previous relationships and experiences. After making our list of possible motives, we look over our list of observations for that person to see if any of them could confirm any of those possible motivations we listed.

It is impossible to know if we have a predisposed bias when looking through our observations of that person. And it is possible to see anything we want to see in the observations when we look at them with a predetermined idea of what we will find. This is truly the most unreliable way to determine another person's motive for one or more of these reasons because:

    a. It is too subjective. When you take counsel only with yourself, you are being counseled by a fool. You have no idea when you are deceiving yourself.

    b. Your list of possible motivations will be influenced by the motivations of previous relationships you have had. This bias makes it impossible for you to be objective in the current relationship.

    c. There is no way for you to have all the facts in the current situation unless you talk to the person whose action you are questioning. Making judgments without having as many of the facts that you possibly can have is a foolish thing to do.

3. We ask a close friend of theirs about the person's motivation.

Usually we do this because we want to believe the best, and hope that, by asking one of their closest friends, they will confirm our hopes and give us their reasons for that hope. We will then use their reasons in our files to validate the concluded motives that they have given us.

In reality, this is a lazy way to arrive at our conclusions. It relies upon someone else to invest time and energy into a relationship with the person we should be investing our time with to get to properly know them.

It's important to note that it is never a healthy practice to clutter our files with data from someone else's files about a person, even if the conclusions are positive. Doing so is gossiping.

4. We probe the files of people who are not close to the person with the questionable action.

Usually we do this because we want to believe the worst about the person, and we're looking for someone to validate that thinking. Our communication with these people will include leading statements suggesting negative motivations to see if the person we're talking to may feel the same way or if they can be swayed to feel that way. If we encounter someone who isn't prone to gossip, we'll cease our communication with them about the person in question and keep looking for someone who is willing to gossip.

When we find someone who believes the worst about the person we are investigating, we gladly populate our questionable actions column with data from their file. We quickly make their conclusions ours and use that to validate our proposed motivations. We use their conclusions as iron-clad proof that we came to the right conclusion, and they use our conclusions about that person in the same way. It is called circular reasoning.

Even though it feels good to our flesh to have someone validate our negative conclusions about someone's motivation, our flesh will never be satisfied with just one verification. This will drive us to continue to search for others who will share our judgment about that person. Gossiping is very addicting.

THE MATTHEW EIGHTEEN PROCESS

The only biblical way to determine someone else's motives is to follow what Jesus taught us in Matthew chapter 18. We talked about the first step of this process before. It is to go to your brother in private and tell him what is troubling you. I know this can be very scary, but according to Jesus, if we have not gone to our brother in private first, we have no right to talk to anyone else about the situation.

Here is the complete process that Jesus taught us for conflict resolution.

> *Moreover if your brother sins against you, go and tell him his fault between you and him alone. If he hears you, you have gained your brother. But if he will not hear, take with you one or two more, that 'by the mouth of two or three witnesses every word may be established.' And if he refuses to hear them, tell it to the church. But if he refuses even to hear the church, let him be to you like a heathen and a tax collector. Matthew 18:15-17 (NKJV)*

I would like for you not to read this as if you are the one who is right and the one you are going to is the offender. Never assume that an offence has occurred. Until you know your brother's motivation, you cannot know if you have the right to be offended or not.

Always approach a questionable action by another as a misunderstanding. Never consider a questionable action as an offense. Remember what Peter Marshall, Jr. taught us: We all have the same capability of being wrong. Rather than approaching your brother and telling him the way he offended you, ask him for clarity of what he meant by what he did or said. You may end up being the one needing to ask for forgiveness. Never assume you are right.

The second stage of this process is to involve one or two other people. Please note, these people are to go with you to talk to the brother with whom you need to be reconciled. This does not mean that you discuss the situation with these other people in private, without the brother being present to hear what you are saying about them. At no time are you to discuss the conflict you have with another brother without that brother being present to hear everything you say. Resist the urge to fill in the background of a conflict without both parties being present. If you do, you are going against this biblical pattern and have gone into gossip and slander.

> *For I am afraid that when I come I may not find you as I want you to be, and you may not find me as you want me to be. I fear that there may be discord, jealousy, fits of rage, selfish ambition, slander, gossip, arrogance and disorder. 2 Corinthians 12:20 (NIV)*

All of these things listed in this verse are what the devil uses against our relationships in the body of Christ. If we see ourselves doing any of them, we know we are not being led by the Spirit of God.

The third step in Matthew's reconciliation process is to bring it before the church. This does not mean that you stand in front of the church and tell everyone how you have been offended. This means that you humble yourself before the church, asking them to pray for you and that your broken relationship will be restored. Do not give any details of the conflict between you and your brother. Maintain the attitude that you could be the one at fault. By bringing this conflict before the church, you and your brother are demonstrating vulnerability and asking the church to pray for this needed resolve. It also tells the church that you are both open to whoever is led by God to speak into your lives.

When you have that many people concerned that the unity of their worship is in jeopardy because of this conflict, they will fervently seek God for a resolve. Traditionally church members take sides with one of the two people who are having a conflict. However, that is not what Jesus wants from us here. The unity in our group worship is far more important than who is right in any given conflict.

The final stage in this process does not say that one of you has to leave the church if a resolution is not reached. It simply says that, you should treat each other like tax collectors. The question is, how do you treat a tax collector? In biblical times, a tax collector would collect taxes from people every time they crossed paths, so most people thought the best way to treat a tax collector was to avoid them. To treat someone like a heathen means to be cordial with them but not spend a lot of time with them. If you cannot be reconciled with your brother, you still need to live in peace with them.

> *If it be possible, as much as lieth in you, live peaceably with all men. Romans 12:18 (KJV)*

I personally believe that a relationship does not have to stay in this state forever. Sometimes we just need a little time for God to work on our hearts and for us to humble ourselves.

I never will forget what a pastor friend said to me when I was talking to him about how offended I was with another pastor in town.

"But I'm right in this situation," I insisted.

"Would you rather be right," he asked me, "or forgiven?"

"But," I started to argue with him. Then I realized he was right. In conflicts and misunderstandings, it really doesn't matter who is right; it only matters that we forgive one another and walk in humility.

Avoiding Offences

We can save ourselves a tremendous amount of stress and conflict by walking in humility and forgiveness toward everyone, especially our Christian brothers and sisters. The way we do that is simple. Whenever an observation becomes a questionable action in anyone's file and before we communicate anything to that person, we write *forgiven* in the motivation column. We forgive them then we communicate with them from a heart full of love.

Here's how their file should look:

People Files #2

Visual Images of the Person:

Name and other pertinent information we learn as the relationship develops:

Event File Link	Observation	Questionable Action	Personal Timer	(Possible) Motivation(s)
			DISABLED	**FORGIVEN**

Table XXIX

Conclusion

Our relationships with our brothers and sisters in Christ are worth every effort it takes to keep them pure before God. Always remember who is behind the offences that occur. It is the devil and his demons who do not want Godly relationships based on forgiveness and humility.

If the enemy can weaken our Christian family relationships, then our worship is rendered ineffective as punishment for him. For the sake of completing our purpose as Christian worshipers, let us all protect our relationships!

BIBLIOGRAPHY

Donne, John. Devotions Upon Emergent Occasions and Several Steps in My Sickness. 1624. https://www.phrases.org.uk/meanings/no-man-is-an-island.html

Elwell, Walter, A., ed. *Baker's Evangelical Dictionary of Biblical Theology.* Grand Rapids: Baker Books, 1996.

Hall, Thomas. T. "Me and Jesus Got Our Own Thing Goin'," *We All Got Together And. . . .* Sony/ATV Music Publishing, 1972.

Luther, Martin. "A Mighty Fortress Is Our God." Translated by Frederick H. Hedge. 1853.

Nee, Watchman. *The Spiritual Man* (Vol. One). New York: Christian Fellowship Publishers, 1977).

Stone, Shamblin. *Biblical Worship.* Bloomington: WestBow Press, 2012.

Stone, Shamblin. *Portrait of a Worshiper.* Bloomington: WestBow Press, 2018.

Strong, James. *Strong's Exhaustive Concordance of the Bible.* Nashville: Abingdon Press, 1890.

Strong, James. *Strong's Exhaustive Concordance of the Bible.* Peabody: Hendrickson Publishers, 2007.

The Holy Bible, King James Version.

The Holy Bible, New King James Version. Nashville: Thomas Nelson, 1982.

The Holy Bible, New International Version. Colorado Springs: Biblica, 2011.

The Holy Bible, New Living Translation. Carol Stream, IL: Tyndale House Publishers, 2015.

The Living Bible. Carol Stream, IL: Tyndale House, 1971.

OTHER BOOKS
by This Author

PORTRAIT OF A WORSHIPER

Every person who has ever lived has wrestled with the question of the purpose of human life. Stone answers that question definitively with the Word of God that mankind's purpose for existence is, ". . . to the praise of His/God's glory," (Ephesians 1:14). Since that is God's purpose for us, the way God has designed and created us has everything to do with us accomplishing that purpose. This book examines in detail how God made us in His likeness and image and how every part of us is necessary to accomplish God's purpose for us. The book

also looks into God's plan to redeem all parts of a human being so that we can fulfill the purpose for which we were created. Finally, this book explains how each part of our humanity functions when we obey God's purpose for our existence and worship Him.

Softcover: 6x9, 270 pages, ISBN: 978-1-97361-3-039
Hardcover: 6x9, 270 pages, ISBN: 978-1-97361-3-046
E-Book: 270 pages, ISBN: 978-1-97361-3-022

BIBLICAL WORSHIP

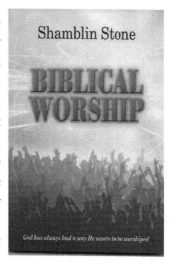

Shamblin Stone

BIBLICAL WORSHIP

God has always had a way He wants to be worshiped

God has always had a way He wants to be worshiped. He has outlined that way for us in His written revelation: the Bible. In it, He has commanded us to worship Him with our entire being, holding nothing back. According to Jesus, this is the first and greatest commandment. The reasons God has given us for obeying His commands to worship Him are because of who He is and because of what He does. Worship is the biblically declared reason for mankind's existence. However, how and when we worship is just as important as the fact that we do worship. Also, it is important to understand God's meaning of the biblical synonyms of worship when we try to obtain a more complete picture of how God wants us to worship Him. *Biblical Worship* is a book for every Christian regardless of their preferred worship style or worship traditions. The fresh, new insights contained within its pages about what type of worship God desires from us all have the potential to shock you at times. At the very least, this book will cause you to never view worship the same way again.

Softcover: 6x9, 162 pages, ISBN: 978-1-44973-7-139
Hardcover: 6x9, 162 pages, ISBN: 978-1-44973-7-146
E-Book: 162 pages, ISBN: 978-1-44973-7-122

FOR MORE WORSHIP RESOURCES
go to

WWW.THEWORSHIPCOLLEGE.COM

- ➢ FREE eight-week Bible class/Sunday school curriculum
- ➢ FREE e-book downloads
- ➢ FREE music downloads
- ➢ Books to purchase
- ➢ CDs and DVDs to purchase
- ➢ Online/video vocal-training course
- ➢ The Tone-Deaf Challenge
- ➢ *The Worship Magazine*